The Occult in Tsarist Russia

By

THOMAS E BERRY, PHD

Strategic Book Publishing and Rights Co.

Strategic Book Publishing and Rights Co.
12620 FM 1960, Suite A4-507
Houston, TX 77065
www.sbpra.com

ISBN: 978-1-61897-691-8

Design: Dedicated Book Services (www.netdbs.com)

Acknowledgements

Research for this study was assisted by:

Librarians in the Vatican Library, Rome

The University of Helsinki Library

The Saltykov-Schedrin Library, St. Petersburg

The New York City Library

The British Museum, London

The Library of Congress, Washington DC

In honor of my father-in-law, Vladimir Anatolievich Kalichevsky, Corps des Pages. Class of 1914

Kamer Page to Her Majesty Alexandra Feodorovna

Table of Contents

Foreword

Witchcraft and Superstitions In Russian History

Occult sciences date back to the earliest periods of Russian science with mediums and spiritualists in society and literature in the latter eighteenth century, but they achieved their fullest development in the middle of the nineteenth century. During the reign of Catherine the Great, mediums became popular and spiritualistic societies developed. While the monarch herself did not believe in spiritualism, she wrote to protest against its practices. The nature of the intelligentsia during her rule encouraged the spread of occult sciences. With the decline of interest in the Russian Orthodox Church among the educated, mysticism became a substitute for traditional religion, much as it was in the West. Catherine deplored the spread of the freemasons and other secretive societies. However, the Russian interest in the spiritual and the intense obsession with spiritualism promoted the séances that were held in fashionable salons by such occultists as Cagliostro. Various forms of spiritualism took hold in Russia during the reign of the Empress and they continued developing until the Revolution of 1917.

It is not well known that many famous Russian writers such as Turgenev, Tolstoy and Dostoevsky attended séances or that Pushkin's family saw ghosts. Spiritualism was much discussed and widely practiced in Russian society and literature. Several tsars and other members of the royal family were followers of the occult science. The occultists and mediums, such as Rasputin and Dr. Philippe, who entered the royal palaces during the reign of Nicholas II were a continuation of a tradition of spiritualism in the imperial family. This tradition had a dual nature. There was always a folk undercurrent that accompanied the Western spiritualism which society accepted as a revelation and which was expressed in Russian literature. During Nicholas II's reign, Rasputin can represent the folk tradition in contrast with the Western spiritualism of Dr. Philippe.

It is interesting that contemporary historians have neglected the Russian preoccupation with spiritualistic and occult matters during the nineteenth century. Scholars have pointed out other aspects of the haunted period: the questioning of religious beliefs brought on by the development of science and psychology and the rise of a social consciousness that led to political radicalism. However, for the most part, the popularity of spiritualism in the later days of imperial Russia has been overlooked. The occult sciences played a role in the fall of the monarchy.

Part I

The Reign of Catherine the Great: Spiritualism in the Rational Eighteenth Century

The Age of Rationalism was not devoid of the irrational; fortune telling with the Bible was popular, mystical sects were formed, séances were held and stories of the supernatural were in demand by the reading public.[1] It was also a century of Pietism, of Young's *Night Thoughts*, and of Swedenborg. Specters and apparitions were seen on all levels of society. Even the enlightened Catherine the Great was supposed to have seen a vision in 1796. Her fantastic experience was reported by the Duke de Doudeauville, but the veracity of the account is subject to doubt:

"On November 2, 1798, the ladies-in-waiting and the door servants of her majesty's bedroom noticed that the empress, dressed in bed clothes and holding a candle, left her bedroom and went in the direction of the throne room. At first they were very surprised at such strange behavior; then they began to worry about her prolonged absence. How much greater was their surprise when they heard the empress's bell from her bedchamber. Rushing into the room, they saw her majesty on her bed. She asked with displeasure what was keeping her from sleeping. The ladies-in-waiting were afraid to tell the truth, but the empress quickly noticed their confusion and soon forced them to tell in detail what had happened. Having shown great interest in the story, the empress ordered that they help her dress; then they escorted her to the throne room. The door was open and a strange light appeared before the eyes of all present. The large hall was lighted by some sort of greenish light. A ghost sat on the throne. The specter was a double of her majesty. The empress screamed and fainted.[2]

Save for the above account of Catherine's experience by the Duke de Doudeauville, no other historical documentation of the incident has appeared. The occurrence certainly does not seem in keeping with the empress's character. Catherine II was known for her strong will and independence. While born a German princess, she strove to identify herself with Russia. She joined the Russian Orthodox Church, learned the Russian language and championed the causes of her new land in military campaigns and domestic reforms. She also corresponded with the leading philosophical writers of the eighteenth century, including Voltaire, Diderot, Grimm and Holbach. Everything in her background suggests that she would not be affected by or even believe in a phenomenon of the sort related above.

According to the journal "Rebus," other Russian monarchs of the eighteenth century saw specters. During the reign of Anna Ivanovna, a spirit was supposed to have arisen from the tomb of Peter the Great. It demanded that the throne be given to the dead monarch's daughter Elizabeth. Tsar Paul Petrovich was also reported a witness to a specter of Peter.[4] These spiritualistic encounters lack documentation and their verisimilitude is in doubt. However, many psychic phenomena were part of this age when even the enlightened were prone to mysticism.

An example of the popularity of mystical matters in the eighteenth century is the debate about witchcraft that took place during Catherine the Great's reign in the well-informed Russian senate in 1769.[5] The judicial body discussed the strange incidents that occurred in the town of Iarenska of the Pechorskii district. It was reported to the senate that witches and sorcerers were appearing among the peasants, turning them from the orthodox faith and infecting many with various illnesses by means of worms. The senate debated the matter and ordered that the men involved to be sent to the army with their wives because the deceit and witchery they were practicing consisted of premeditated designs on the health of others. However, before the decision reached Iarenska, the Holy Synod announced that such affairs were under its jurisdiction. While the fate of the Iarenska witches is lost in history the incident shows the persistence of a belief in the supernatural, a Russian folk tradition, while the highest realms of society had pretensions of Western European enlightenment.

In 1769, M. Chulkov published a *Dictionary of Russian Superstitions* which, as he mentioned in the frontispiece, was designed "to show those superstitions worthy of laughter and destroy them, if it is possible." Chulkov's definition of witches incorporates into one group the following types: sorcerers, wizards, fortune tellers, black-magicians and soothsayers. It also attempts to show the absurdity of any belief in the occult creatures: "Such ones can deal with people, give them diseases or spoil them. When they die they leave a magic book to one of their relatives. If someone finds such a book and starts reading it, immediately a multitude of devils will appear and ask for tasks. If they are not heeded, the reader will be killed."

Chulkov's dictionary became so popular; a second expanded edition was published in 1789.[6]

In the eighteenth century, the superstitious nature of the Russian ruling class encouraged the visit and assured the success of many European mediums, occultists and charlatans. Their achievements and popularity set the stage for the great onslaught of Western mediums in the nineteenth century. Among the noted mediums to visit Russia in the eighteenth century were Cagliostro and the Comte de St. Germaine. The latter was reported to have been in Russian court circles and he was even supposed to have helped Catherine II in the takeover of the Russian throne. However, the mystical Comte de St. Germaine's presence in Russia has never been documented.[7] The other occultist, Cagliostro, certainly did visit Russia where he was responsible for a very negative literary outpouring by the Empress Catherine II.

In 1779, the famous medium and empiricist Cagliostro set out for St. Petersburg expecting an appreciative reception from Russian society. As a doctor, alchemist and rumored possessor of life-prolonging elixirs, Cagliostro was counting on finding followers among the highest spheres of society in the Russian capital as he had in other European citadels. As a magician and spiritualist, the thought he would easily find adherents. He was also sure, as a Mason, that he would find support among the many Masonic lodges that had spread throughout Russia. His ambition even extended to the Empress Catherine II whom he hoped to make one of his disciples.[8] However, he did not know that his assumptions about Russian society and the monarch were more imaginary than realistic. Catherine said about his visit, "He pretends to be a master sorcerer, seeing spirits who await his commands. When I heard all this, I remarked that he made a great mistake in coming here. Nowhere will he score less than in Russia where there is no enthusiasm for sorcerers,"[9]

The Empress had considerable disdain for the esoteric.[10] In the poem "Felitsa," which brought G. R. Derzhavin fame, the poet described Catherine as the monarch "who did not attend séances."[11] The empress was too much of an eighteenth century rationalist to give credence to anagoges. She abhorred the spread of Masonic lodges in Russia and as early as 1759 wrote a tract entitled "Le Secret de la Societé Anti-Absurde," in which she made fun of Masonic rites. While this tract was not made public until 1780,[12] it was no doubt passed among the court circles of the time because it was known that the empress was very critical of the Masonic movement.

After a short time in St. Petersburg, Cagliostro sensed his own lack of importance in the Russian capital. However, he did not try to increase his standing in society by resorting to advertising himself as other mediums did in the *St. Petersburg Vedomosti*. That paper often had exaggerated claims advertised by occultists; for instance, one French medium claimed that he could heal various diseases including the consequences from a "blow of air."[13] Cagliostro considered himself above such advertising and relied on word of mouth to spread his reputation. He held small séances and bragged about his ability to cure various diseases. His ability did bring him considerable fame.

When Prince G. V. Golitsin turned to Cagliostro for help during the illness of the prince's infant son, Cagliostro took advantage of the aristocrat's concern and set up a scheme that guaranteed success.[14] The infant heir to the prestigious family was considered beyond hope by leading doctors in the city. The prince and princess were in despair. Cagliostro claimed he would cure the child if the upper-class couple would agree to the following conditions: they had to allow him to take the infant to his apartment and not visit him until he informed them that it was suitable. As much as they did not want to part with their son, the couple agreed. After two weeks, the doctor-medium allowed the prince to see the improvement the child was making. Finally the infant went home completely cured. The grateful prince offered Cagliostro a thousand gold imperials, but he refused. The miraculous cure and the medium's refusal to take such an exorbitant sum soon spread throughout the capital. Finally the prince offered Cagliostro five thousand gold imperials and Cagliostro did not refuse them.

After several days the princess Golitsin began to suspect a deception. She feared that her child had been substituted with another. The suspicion had a weak basis, but nevertheless the story spread all over the city. In a book by a servant of Cagliostro, it was reported that the son of the princess was exchanged with a healthy infant and that the charlatan admitted making the switch so that the young mother would not suffer. When asked what he did with the prince's son when it died, the medium reported that he burned it.[15]

Cagliostro also achieved prominence by using his beautiful young wife Lorenze in his séances. In conversations with clients she would talk about her husband's amazing powers. She maintained that he was over a hundred years old and that she herself was forty. They stayed young because of a miraculous elixir which Cagliostro began selling for enormous sums. Some of those that did not believe in the elixir did accept the charlatan's ability to turn base metals into gold. For instance, State Secretary Elagin became Cagliostro's pupil and enhanced the medium's reputation.[16]

In spite of his limited success in the Russian capital, Cagliostro was never able to achieve his goal of winning any support from Catherine the Great. The Empress actually despised him and wrote two plays, "The Charlatan" and "The Deceiver," about his activities. It has been assumed that she was responsible for his early departure from St. Petersburg.

Several reasons have been given for Catherine's animosity against Cagliostro. One of the major causes could have been the medium's link to the Masons whom the Empress hated. The major Masonic lodges of the time were in Moscow and the St. Petersburg Masons were eager to be initiated into the highest orders of the cult. Cagliostro's claims to the highest orders and his knowledge of the Masonic rites could have caused him to be accepted by the Masons, thereby insuring the wrath of the ruler. In her play, "The Trompeur," Catherine gave Cagliostro the name Kalifalkgerston and had him talking with spirits in a Masonic rite while he robbed those for whom he was performing.

Another cause of the hatred of Catherine for the medium might have been the attention that her lover General Potemkin paid to Cagliostro's wife Lorenza. It was rumored that the famous statesman was captivate by the medium's spouse and that Catherine was furious when she found out. Cagliostro's stay in St. Petersburg was supposedly shortened because of the empress' anger.[17] However, his exit from the city was done according to the laws of the time. A foreigner was required in those days to publish the date of his departure in the *St. Petersburg Vedomosti* three times before he was granted permission to leave. Cagliostro's name appeared the first time on October 1, 1779, in number 79 of the gazette. It was also in numbers 80 and 81.[18] Whatever the cause of the medium's departure, his stay in the capital must have been considerably shorter and less successful than he had intended.

Catherine the Great and Esoteric Literature

While Catherine II wrote plays deriding spiritualism and the medium Cagliostro, the empress was not alien to fantasy in her other writings. After the translation of the *One Thousand and One Nights* in 1763, a new world opened for Russian writers.[19] Eastern tales had already influenced medieval folk tales,[20] but the translation of the Arabian stories presented new themes. Fantasy was blended with reality in dramas, poetry and prose. Catherine furthered the development of occult tales in her own literary endeavors. Her comic-operas and historical dramas were based on Russian fairy tales, myths and historical songs. She also used indirect comments on contemporary situations in the tradition of Montesquieu's "Persian Letters."

In her "A Fairy Tale about Prince Khlor," the Empress imitated the French fairy tale, "Florine ou la belle Italienne, nouveau conte de Fées."[21] While she borrowed some supernatural aspects from the French story, for instance, the "rose without prickles that stings not" and the "bagpipe that lures," she toned down the setting of the story from the "Land of the Fairies" to an exotic Eastern setting at the court of a Khan. Prince Khlor was no longer guarded by "magical charms" as in the French story, but by "seven nannies" in the empress' version.

Catherine, however, was capable of highly imaginative writing. In her "Fairy Tale about the Woe-begone Knight Kosometovich," various humorous situations were described. The Don Quixote-type knight had trouble selecting the horse for his pilgrimage and his sword had to be shortened so that he could take it out of its halter. Catherine's fairy tales made fantasy acceptable in the most rational court circles.

Russian Society and Anagogic Literature

Writers followed Catherine's example and turned to fairy tales and spiritualism for subject matter. Fantasy tales became so popular that the serious writer N.I. Novikov, complained about the taste of the Russian reading public and gave a warning for the future,[22] "Who in France would have thought that *Eastern Fairy Tales* would have a greater distribution than the works of Racine? And what has happened here? *The One Thousand and One Nights* is sold more than Sumarokov. And what London bookseller would not have been horrified after hearing that sometimes here 200 copies of a printed book have not been sold in the course of ten years. Oh, such times! Oh, morality! Russian writer, come to your senses, your compositions will soon not be bought at all."

The writers of classical compositions whose books were not "sold in the course of ten years" also complained against the spread of fanciful literature. A.F. Sumarokov, noted for his classical plays, railed against the spread of fanciful novels and explained their popularity: "They have little purpose, and are quite harmful. It is said that such literature takes away boredom and helps pass away time, which is short enough without such help! . . . It is said that such literature serves as a comfort to the uneducated because other books are not understandable to them."[23]

Concern over the public's taste caused the appearance of a tract entitled "The Danger of Reading Fantasy Novels," in which there was the following warning: "O, dear kind women! You, whom nature awarded such a sensitive soul. Guard yourself as much as possible from reading dangerous novels, especially those that are becoming so pleasing to us now."[24]

Another classicist, M.M. Kheraskov, condemned fanciful works in 1760 with the following remarks: "Oh, weak compositions!" Wisdom shouted. "Do you deserve to occupy a place in this world? Have you not deformed nature and made meaning senseless? You are nothing but something that can cause harm; or even better, you are a travesty to all mankind."[25] Kheraskov, however, did change his mind and later wrote fanciful works according to the public's taste.

The first Russian fantasy novel with spirits, walking corpses and fays was M. Chulkov's *The Mocker of Slavic Fairy Tales*, written in 1766.[26] In the foreword to the book, the author admitted that there was "little value or moral teaching in the book, actually none at all. It is not useful, it seems to me, for correcting morals; so, leaving that aside, it will be useful for passing time . . . I am trying to be a writer and if only that will happen someday."[27]

Several Russian anagogic tales were inspired by the noted French philosopher Voltaire who corresponded with Catherine II. The French writer laughed at the absurd elements of tales where "fairies ran through castles" and "every village had its sorcerer and every prince his astrologer."[28] However, the author did use the esoteric in his works. His "Micromegas," which described travel in other inhabited planets, appeared in Russian in 1759 and inspired other writers to venture into outer space; for instance, "The Gentleman-Philosopher" by F. Dmitriev-Mamonov and "The Newest Journey" by V. Levskin.

Political satire based on the esoteric also became popular. Apparitions and devils soon entered literary stylization. In 1769 F. Emin began publishing *The Devil's Post*, a journal that recorded the conversations of two devils, Mr. Crooked and Mr. Snores.[29] Their comments were often witty: "Mr. Crooked: The more I deal with people, the more I find their personal qualities to be strange." (Letter 56) "Mr. Snores, my friend, when you realize that a man cannot be a devil and a devil can never be man, then you will not be surprised." (Letter 57)

Subjects were often given light treatment by the two letter-writing devils; for instance, in a discussion on utilitarianism, Mr. Crooked says: "You said that 'science and art will have respect by the public when they have some use.' How can you praise a writer who wrote about which end a fly breathes from, or whether fleas jump straight or crooked, or how bees measure their hives without a compass. Don't such men deserve respect?" (Letter 59)

Mr. Snores replies, "Scholars and thinking men are not necessarily the same." (Letter 60) The droll comments by Mr. Snores were often political barbs, which the censors of Catherine the Great did not appreciate and the journal was closed after six months.[30]

Another short lived journal based on spiritualistic themes was *The Post Office of Spirits* created by I. Krylov in 1789.[31] The publication presented the correspondence between the witch Malikulmulka and several nymphs, gnomes and undines who lived among people and observed their lives. In Letter 1, from the gnome, Zora, to the witch, the upper-class' taste for French fashion was criticized:[31] "So I'd better tell you the news. What horrible changes there have been in Hell! Proserpine returned from a half-year's absence. Pluto awaited her return with impatience . . . the goddess came in wearing the latest French dress, a hat with feathers and beautiful shoes with heels that raised her three times her height. Poor Pluto turned to stone when he saw her attire . . . Several of us very politely said, 'She's lost her mind!'"[32]

Krylov's fanciful letters were printed monthly for nine months before the writer gave in to governmental pressure to stop the journal. The author's political and social jibes had become too blatant.

As fanciful literature with spirits, sorcerers and specters increased in popularity, some writers published their works anonymously. For instance, on the Frontispiece of the romantic fantasy "Dobrala the Sorceress" in 1789, the unknown author said, "I want to produce something useful, morally instructive, and simple, but that won't give me any profit."[33] Later he characterized successful Russian literature as "daring idleness, expressed with simple mindedness: old thoughts in a new setting, dressed up in new expressions to capture whoever reads them: false rules decorated with the same philosophy, a riff-raff of daring lies, presented as reality."[34] While fanciful Russian literature of the latter eighteenth century had little literary value, it did acquaint the public with supernatural themes and opened the way for an appreciation of Romantic literature from the West. Already toward the end of the century the novels of Walpole and Radcliffe were bringing Romantic sentiment and Gothic stylization to Russian literature.

In 1798 a French émigré printed in the "Sectateur du Nord" the following recipe for a horror novel:

1. Take one old castle, half in ruins
2. Several long hallways with a few hidden doors
3. Three wounded corpses, still bleeding

4. An old hag with dagger stabs in her throat
5. Thieves, as many as you wish
6. Douse with moaning and shrieks.[35]

The French parodist satirized Gothic stylization at a time when the genre was well-known in Europe. In Russia, however, original Gothic tales were rare in the latter eighteenth century even though some translations of Gothic novels had appeared.

N.M. Karamzin published a Gothic tale, *The Island of Bornholm* in 1794,[36] The same year Ann Radcliffe's *The Mysteries of Udolpho* appeared. Karamzin was probably familiar with her Gothic novels *The Sicilian Romance* (1790) and *The Romance of the Forest* (1791). However, his only reference to the English author was in his essay "Historical Remembrances and Notes on the Way to the Monastery of the Holy Trinity" in 1803. The sacred place dated from the time of Ivan the Terrible and Karamzin wrote that "Mrs. Radcliffe could have used the building for a horror novel."[37] The writer found everything for a Gothic novel: empty halls, corridors, high staircases, remnants of splendorous decorations and banging doors.

While there is no record that Karamzin read Radcliffe's novels, his own Gothic stories sometimes followed her style. He usually explained away his mysteries àla Radcliffe; for instance, in his story "The Deep Forest," in 1794, he explained a monster's flames by sparks and campfires. [38] Yet in his story "The Island of Bornholm" he did not follow the English writer's practice of giving a realistic explanation for the mysterious. The heroine of the story revealed the details of her distressing situation to an old man and not to the reader. Karamzin had learned that Gothic mysteries wane when explained. However, "The Island of Bornholm" caused considerable concern among the reading public. A.T. Bolotov, a contemporary now noted for his memoirs, waited naively for a sequel to Karamzin's story.[39] And the Dowager Empress Maria Fedorovna asked about the fate of the heroine as late as 1815.[40]

While there were few Russian Gothic writers in the latter eighteenth century, foreign Gothic literature became very popular in Russia in the nineteenth century. Ghosts and specters became widespread in literature after the Napoleonic Wars and séances and mediums soon became the rage. It was the interest in fanciful literature and the spread of mysticism in religious rites during the reign of Catherine the Great that prepared the way for the widespread development of spiritualism in Russia in the nineteenth century.

Part II

The Reign of Alexander I: Spiritualism at the Royal Court

Because of the enigmatic character of Tsar Alexander I, an aura of mysticism prevailed during his reign at the beginning of the nineteenth century.[1] Reared in the enlightened court of his grandmother, Catherine the Great, the liberally inclined young tsar became engrossed with a religious fervor early in his rule due to the spiritualistic interests of the people who surrounded him. Several of his state ministers, such as M. Speransky,[2] A. Golitsin,[3] and A. Arakcheev[4] professed anagogic doctrines and a number of mystics had an influence on Alexander. For instance, the tsar enjoyed the company of a Madame Krudener who predicted his future,[5] and he took a keen interest in rites held in the apartments of the Countess Tatarinov.[6] An account of one of her ceremonies was left by F. F. Vigil, a former district governor whose memoirs give a detailed view of court life, including his own perverted interests. While visiting in the Mikhailovsky Palace, Vigil heard strange sounds. He looked out a window into a lower wing of the palace complex and saw the following: "Countess Tatarinov sat on a chair in the middle of the floor. Men sat around the sides of the walls and women stood before her, expecting a sign. When she gave it, they began to whirl while the men sang and beat their knees louder and louder. The rotating women turned into spinning tops . . . The crashing together of two of the fanatics was horrible.[7]

Alexander's interest in séances and cults such as the Countess Tatarinov's was due in part to his education at the court of the illustrious Catherine II. Disillusioned with her own son Paul, who had been taken from her as a child and reared by the Empress Elizabeth, Catherine decided to create a capable tsar from one of her grandsons.[8] Following the example of her predecessor, she took the future Alexander I from his mother and closely attended to his education. She was determined that he would not be like her son Paul, a weakling with a militaristic bent and stubborn character. A great admirer of Western culture and philosophy, the empress imported Monsieur La Harpe as tutor for her grandson.[9] The teacher was from Switzerland and was imbued with Eastern liberalism. He gave Alexander studies in governmental theory and classical literature. Lofty concepts prevailed, but as the historian Strakhovsky noted, there was little of educational value passed on to the student.[10] The tsarevich's ability to think logically and practically was left undeveloped. Consequently, in maturity he was inclined to interpret the Bible literally. In his opinion the holy book offered easy, uncomplicated solutions and many of the Biblical passages seemed to apply directly to many of his problems. The tsar came to the conclusion that God was directing him through the printed word.[11] Alexander lacked the insights and judgment that were needed for the particular role he was to play in history.

One of the greatest influences on the young tsar was his friendship with Prince Alexander Nikolaevich Golitsyn. The latter was accepted by Catherine the Great as a playmate for her grandsons Alexander and Constantine through the influence of a lady-in-waiting, Maria Svishna Perekusikhina, a friend of Golitsyn's mother.[12] By the empress' order, Glitsyn became a page of the court and was allowed to play with the future tsar during holidays. The two young men grew up as close friends. When the Emperor Paul came to the throne, he approved of the relationship between the two friends, but when Golitsyn once provoked the wrath of the ruler, he was forced to leave the city and move to Moscow. In the former capital the newcomer studied in the private library of Count Buturlin.[13] It was during this period that the exiled young man became a follower of the liberal ideas of Voltaire.

In 1804 Alexander, now tsar, called his friend to St. Petersburg where he was designated pro-curator of the Holy Synod. Golitsyn accepted the position only after he received permission to report personally to the tsar about the affairs of the new office. Such an exception had never been granted before, but the monarch agreed.[14] Accepting the position, Golitsyn tried to become familiar with basic church doctrine. He read the Old Testament for the first time. Under the influence of his studies and position, he began to give up the pleasures and entertainments that had been his major interest. It is assumed that during this period he also directed his friend Alexander's interests to Biblical and spiritualistic studies. One incident in their relationship at this time showed the tsar's susceptibility to outward influence. During the occupation of Moscow by Napoleon, Golitsyn encouraged his friend to rely on the Bible for direction. When they looked at the holy book, it was opened to the 91st Psalm, which spoke of seeking refuge in the Lord. Alexander was impressed by the text, but he became convinced of its significance when he heard the same verses in a service a few days later.[15] The tsar decided that the coincidence was a sign from God that the Bible could answer governmental problems. From his reading, he concluded that he was the savior of Europe and that Napoleon was the antichrist.

Alexander had associated the French Emperor with the Biblical antichrist once before. In 1805 he consulted with a religious mystic name Kondratit Sevastianov who was considered a prophet by his large following of religious zealots. The tsar received some sobering predictions. He was told that "his hour had not yet come" and that Napoleon "as the enemy of mankind" would defeat the Russian army.[16] The tsar did experience the shame of defeat at Austerlitz and had waited for years to destroy Napoleon. Remembering Sevastianov's words about his "time" in the future, Alexander decided that God was communicating with him through the Bible and that his "time" had finally come.

When Napoleon's armies began their retreat from Moscow, Alexander seized the moment against the advice of his family and generals to begin a campaign against the antichrist across the pathways of Europe. He was sure of the righteousness of his crusade and was ready to show Europe his new role as the savior of mankind. However, he did not impress Europeans in the way he intended. Instead, his religious fervor caused astute politicians to consider him naïve.

During the campaign toward France, an incident occurred at the Battle of Dresden which made Alexander proclaim that he was under divine protection. While watching the conflict from a hillock, the tsar noticed that his horse was continually beating the ground where a shoe had struck a stone. Alexander moved his animal a few feet to the side. At that moment General Moreau rode up alongside the Emperor and occupied the spot where the tsar's horse had been standing. In seconds an enemy shot hit the general and he was mortally wounded. The suddenness of the event made a great impression on the astounded tsar and he was convinced of God's intervention on his behalf.[17] In a sense it was the Russian folk spirit that was to direct him in overwhelming Napoleon's trained and disciplined forces.

The Russian folk tradition was soon joined with Western spiritualism, continuing the tradition from Catherine's reign. In his religious fervor Alexander was certainly open to outside influence and it is understandable how he was attracted to the spiritualistic activities of the notorious Baroness Krudener. During the final campaign of the ruler's great crusade, the Battle of Waterloo, the tsar experienced depression and longed for spiritual guidance. To his amazement his aid, Prince Volkonskii, appeared with a message that the noted spiritualist Baroness Krudener wished an audience with him. The tsar was amazed by the suddenness and strangeness of her appearance and he welcomed her enthusiastically.[18] She became his constant companion, discussing the Bible with him for hours. The baroness related to the Swiss Reverend Empatyz, who accompanied her on her missions, that the tsar had confessed his sinfulness and had wept openly over several passages of the Bible. He was very eager to seek salvation and together they had read the Bible for guidance. The companionship between the emperor and the spiritualist continued for weeks. She accompanied him back to Paris and occupied rooms adjoining the royal suite in a French palace. Her influence on the monarch was considerable, not only in his personal life, but also in his governmental plans.[19]

When Alexander went to the Congress of Vienna for the final treaties of the Napoleonic Wars, the Baroness Krudener was in the tsar's entourage. The famous Austrian statesman Metternich considered the baroness as a possible source for the Russian ruler's famous plan for a European alliance. While the ministers of France, England and Austria were highly skeptical of the tsar's visionary plan, they humored him because of his powerful, position and because his naiveté was by then well known. Metternich himself said, "The Holy Alliance was made neither to restrain the rights of the assembled nor to establish absolutism in any form whatever; it was simply an expression of the Emperor Alexander's mystical feelings or an application of the principles of Christianity to politics."

The Austrian statesman was certainly correct in the latter judgment. Alexander's religious spirit allowed him to be all forgiving and he did not demand any commitments from France as a revenge for the Moscow invasion two years previously. It is possible that Madame Krudener played a role in the tsar's behavior because she had become not only his confidante, but also a member of the royal set. She was given the position of lady-in-waiting to Alexandrine Sturdza, a lady-of-honor to the empress.

Spiritualists were very popular in Russia after the Napoleonic Wars and their impact can be seen in the development of Russian letters. A.F. Labzin created the journal *The Herald of Zion* in 1806 and published thirty booklets on Masonry that were very popular.[21] M.I. Nevzorov started the journal *A Friend of Youth* and wrote one of the popular travel books of the time, *A Trip to Kazan, Viatka, and Orenburg*.[22] I.V. Lopukhin published articles in the mystical journals and held high positions in the government.[23] Yet the noted mystics often had to defend their philosophy against the criticism of more rational writers. For instance, when Karl von Eckartshausen's theosophical tract on Phosphorus was translated by Labzin in 1811, critics said that the chemical treatise was ruined by religious interpretations. Nevzorov wrote a defense of the scientific study in "A Friend of Youth." He maintained that Eckartshausen could understand the secrets of nature better than scientists "because he was a good Christian."[24] The reasoning of the mystics was often farfetched. Lokhvitskii wrote that Napoleon was Apollo and used the number of letters in his name to create the "mystical number 666"[25] which is mentioned in the Bible (John, 13:8) L.N. Tolstoy later used the same number in *War and Peace*. Taking note of the strong interest in spiritualism of the period, he described Pierre Bezhkov's susceptibility to the prevalence of the occult science at the time of Napoleon's invasion. In Book III, Part I, Chapter 19, the famous writer tried to belittle the Masons by having a member explain to Pierre Bezukov a number system which proved that Napoleon was the beast prophesied in the Apocalypse.

Mystical organizations were also popular in Russia in the beginning of the nineteenth century. The Masons[26] continued their influence and their journals, *The Herald of Zion27* (1810) and *A Friend of Youth28* (1813) helped spread mysticism during Alexander I's reign. The "Illuminati" claimed 2000 members at the beginning of the nineteenth century in their struggle to exchange Christianity with deism.[29] Yet the greatest influence on Alexander during this period probably came from the Bible Society of St. Petersburg, headed by the tsar's friend Prince A.N. Golitsyn.[30]

In 1819 the British Bible Society sent agents to Finland where they hoped to open a branch of their organization.

The Reverend Peterson traveled to St. Petersburg and met with Prince A. Golitsyn, the director of Russian spiritual affairs. The Englishman had a heart-warming reception in the Russian capital, which resulted in the opening of a Biblical group in St. Petersburg. With the permission of the Emperor, the Bible Society was organized on December 6, 1812, and had its first meeting in the home of Prince Golitsyn on January 11, 1813.[31] At the first gathering, men of all Christian faiths attended. Several Protestants, Catholics and Russian Orthodox officials met and elected the host, Prince Golitsyn, as their president. Two vice-presidents were chosen: V.P. Kochubei and count A.K. Razumovskii, the minister of education.

The Bible Society of St. Petersburg had several aims. It pledged to make the Bible, only recently published in the Holy Synod, more accessible to readers, especially to the poor, the war veterans and the prisoners in Russian jails. The holy book was to be printed in other languages for the benefit of Mohammedans and tribes in remote Russian areas. The members of the Bible Society agreed to buy Bibles and distribute them as cheaply as possible. Emperor Alexander himself pledged 25,000 rubles to the project with an additional 10,000 rubles each succeeding year.[32]

To establish itself, the society had brochures published in 1813 entitled "About the Biblical Society" and "The Branch Institution in St. Petersburg." The success of the advertisements resulted in the opening of six new societies throughout Russia, including a group in Moscow. All the societies collected 160,494 rubles in 1813 alone. In 1815, discussions began on the translation of the Bible from Church Slavonic to contemporary Russian. With the tsar's approval the translation was begun and in 1818 the first parts of the work were published.[33]

While the Bible Society was growing under the directorship of the tsar's friend Prince Golitsyn, much opposition to the prince's policies was also developing. The president of the organization was considered to be too liberal by the officials of the Russian Orthodox Church. Golitsyn did show much tolerance of other religions. He made no effort to subdue other Christians to the Russian Church and even introduced laws that protected Protestants. He also put down any protest that was made against spiritualists and mystics. In time various figures rose in protest to his activities as head of Russian Spiritual Affairs and president of the Bible Society.[34]

Two incidences occurred which showed the rise of powerful conservatives who opposed the liberal policies of Golitsyn. In 1819 M. L. Magnitsky was sent as an inspector general to the University of Kazan. He was astounded at the godless direction of the university. His report, which reflected on Golitsyn who had been Minister of Education, expressed concern about the lack of religious training in the institution. As a result of his investigation, several professors were expelled, Roman law was replaced with the study of Byzantine law, and religious training was made the subject of first importance in the university.[35] In 1831, another occurrence struck closer to Golitsyn's position of power. After attending the lectures the University of St. Petersburg, D.P. Runich sued the educational institution for its anti-religious lectures and principles. As a result, five professors were dismissed.[36]

The Russian Orthodox Church was very suspicious of the new Bible Society from its very beginning. The church officials did not want the Russian Bible in the hands of alien groups such as Catholics and Protestants. The translating of the Bible from Slavonic to Russian was also questioned because it was not being done by the church but by private means. The greatest objection, however, was the strong governmental support the society received. Church dignitaries were alarmed at the growing power of the organization and were especially critical of Prince Golitsyn. Since the tsar was becoming more conservative during the early 1820s, the church leaders turned to him for support of their opposition. Archimandrite Photius, a protégé of a religious fanatic, the Countess Anna Orlov, and a willing minion of the minister of war, the dissolute and vindictive Alexis Arakcheev, went to the tsar in a campaign against mysticism. He linked the liberal policies of the Bible Society with a revolutionary movement and turned the royal mind to his will.[37] In 1824, Alexander asked Prince Golitsyn not to accept the presidency of the Bible Society again and also to step down as head of the Ministry of Spiritual Affairs. The loyal servant and friend of the ruler agreed and gave up his positions to accept the headship of the Post Office department.[38]

While Prince Golitsyn had incurred the wrath of the Russian Church for his liberal tendencies, his handling of literary censorship was certainly in line with the conservative forces in the country. As minister of education in 1816, Golitsyn used a stern hand in dealing with the press and publishers. He prohibited any discussion in print of government activities without the permission of the minister of the department concerned and encouraged private persons not to write on political topics, negatively or positively. Russian letters were in a formative stage after the literary and language reforms of Nicholas Karamzin and his younger and more talented contemporaries, V.A. Zhukovsky and A.S. Pushkin. Censorship, perhaps, played a role in limiting the development of literature during this period, but the rise of the bourgeoisie had increased the demand for light reading and the spread of mysticism had encouraged esoteric literature. Censorship did not hinder the publication of a great number of foreign works, such as the Gothic novels of Ann Radcliffe, and Russian literature, whether as a result of political censorship or the mysticism of the times, gradually followed the example of the imported literature and developed its own spirits, ghosts and romantic stylization. The great interest in mediums and spiritualists in Russian society during the rest of the nineteenth century was reflected in the esoteric and anagogic themes of Russian literature.

The Russian reading public's interest in the supernatural and spiritualism can be seen in the great number of books that were published under the name of Ann Radcliffe from the turn of the century to 1820. Not all of the books printed under her name were translations of her works. Russian authors listed their own works under the English writer's name for the purpose of more sales and perhaps to hide their own identity. Sometimes the Russian writer merely revised a Radcliffe novel, for instance, in 1802 the book *Julia or the Underground Cave of Madzini* was merely a reworking of Radcliffe's *Sicilian Romance* (1790). The following books were printed under the English writer's name after the turn of the century:

The Vision in the Castle of Priren (1802)
The Secrets of Udolfo (1802
The Italian or the Confession of a Penitent (1802)
The Midnight Bell (1802)
The Forest or the Monastery of Satini Clair (1802)
The Castle of Albert (1803)
The Live Corpse (1803)

The Castle or Nighttime Apparitions (1808)
Horrors and Adventures in the Castle of Priren (1809)
Maria and Count M-v or the Misfortunate Girl (1810)
Nighttime Vision (1811)
The Secrets of the Dark Tower (1811)
The Monastery of Saint Catherine (1815)
The Monastery of Saint Columbus (1816)
The Heir of Montalda (1818)
The Cave of Death in a Deep Forest (1818)
The Hermit of the Secret Tomb (1818)
Luisa or the Dungeon of the Castle of Lyon (1819)

Only four of the above books were actual translations of Radcliffe's novels, but the long list of books published under her name certainly indicated the Russian reading public's interest in the esoteric. That interest was carried over into Russian literature which was developing during the early nineteenth century. Mysticism and the supernatural played a considerable role in the early stage of modern Russian literature.

In 1802, A. Izmailov published the first Russian novel that had a touch of the esoteric. In book three, chapter four of his book, *Eugene or the Pernicious consequences of a Poor Upbringing*, the hero, Razvrat, abused an old man and the author interjected his own condemnation: "Curse such heartless ones!" In the next chapter, the writer fulfilled the curse. During a dance, Eugene fell and hurt a foot so badly that he was unable to walk. When he told his companion that he was punished by God "for teasing an old man," the friend laughed and replied, "Well, I conducted myself badly and God did not punish me!" He made the remark while throwing his hands open widely. During the robust gesture, he hit three fingers so hard on a table that he squealed in pain and cursed folly. The remarkable coincidence had supernatural implications: a curse, defiance of God, and the intervention of a higher power.

Gothic stylization was evident in the book *A Russian Gil Blas* (1814) by V.T. Narezhny. In chapter six of part two, the hero, Insandrov excited the reader with the following, "Imagine my surprise when I heard my sigh answered with heavy breathing . . . A frost flowed over my heart. Something white and small . . . stood a short distance from the door . . . The specter . . . moved slowly toward me, reached out its hand and said with tenderness, 'Why are you holding a gun, dear friend?' I glanced and saw . . . my pretty Daria." It was not a vision; it was the author's hackneyed means of gaining attention. And once was not enough. In the same chapter the girl's mother entered the room in the same attire and was called the "second specter." Later when the hero was in a cemetery, he heard a third specter who also turned out to be a young girl. Trite as the literary technique was, it was used by other writers in the 1830s.

A more serious approach to specters and spirits came in the romantic poems of V.A. Zhukovsky, "Liudmila" (1803), "The Ballad of the Old Woman" (1814), "Twelve Sleeping Maidens" (1914), and "Donika" (1830). The first ballad "Liudmila" introduced the vampire into Russian literature at a time when there was a vampire rage in Europe. The interest in the creatures had developed slowly in the eighteenth century. Two literary studies concerning vampires were well known in fashionable salons: the "Dissertatio de Vampiris" (1733) by John Heinrich Zopfius and the "Traits sur les Apparitions des Espirits, et sur les Vampires" (1746) by Dom Calmet.[41] After G.A. Burger wrote "Lenore" in 1773, vampires became very popular in literary fiction all over Europe. Goethe wrote "The Bride of Corinth" (1797); Byron "The Giaour;" Pushkin "The Songs of the Western Slavs," and in 1819 a play, "Le Vampire" by Charles Nodier, packed theaters in Paris.[42]

The noted critic V.G. Belinsky wrote that Zhukovsky "introduced a literary mysticism which consisted of the visionary combined with false fantasy."[43] Zhukovsky's early romantic works continued the major traits of eighteenth century supernatural literature: mysticism and folk themes, such as fate and the intervention of a higher power. His esoteric literature did not have the one aspect that made the difference between eighteenth and nineteenth century fantastic literature: the idealism of the German philosopher F.W.J. von Schelling, which was to enter Russian literature through the stories of the German writer E.T.A. Hoffman during the 1820s and 1830s.[44]

With the success of Zhukovsky's spiritualistic ballads, other writers followed the poet's example. In 1819 K.N. Batiushkov wrote "The Specter" and A.E. Voeikov wrote a satire in 1814 entitled "The House of the Insane" in which every major writer of the period was teased about his style of writing. Zhukovsky was presented as the poet who heckled the devil in his scripts and whose witches always winked at the reader. Batiushkov was pictured in a cage looking into a can of water, saying, "The view above is peaceful, below a terrible crocodile is lying."[45] The peace of heaven and the horrors of earth were popular themes in early romantic literature.

The most famous writer of the period, A.S. Pushkin, not only used spiritualistic images in his works, but also had a family history that resembled a ghost story. Several members of his family had numerous encounters with specters. His grandmother Nadezhda Osipovna was visited three times by a phantom-lady in a white dress at five year intervals. Once as she was walking along the Nevsky Prospect, she turned to her husband and asked, "Do you see the white lady walking beside me?"[46] He didn't. five years later the same apparition appeared in Nadezhda's bedroom only to return again five years later to inform the old woman that she wouldn't be bothered anymore.[47] The spirit did not return, but the Pushkin family never doubted the verisimilitude of the accounts of the recurring specter.

Other members of the Pushkin family were also having psychic visitations. Pushkin's other grandmother Maria Alexseevna Gannibal saw a double of Sergei Lvovich, Pushkin's father, at a name-day party when he was actually ill in bed.[48] Another relative, Pushkin's brother Lev Sergeevich, saw his grandmother in 1826 even though she had died in 1819.[49] She came to him in a shadowy form and blessed him. Later he claimed that in battle bullets missed him as if he were charmed.[50] While these events might seem unbelievable, the Pushkin family did accept them. Pushkin did not ridicule spiritualism; in fact, his works abound with specters and apparitions.

While in the lyceum, Pushkin created several literary apparitions. In the poem "Bova" (1814), the specter that appeared to the heroine Zoya was humane and had a sense of humor. It quieted the girl's fears and admitted that it enjoyed frightening people. In the poem "Epistle to Judin" (1815), the apparition of a loved one followed the author and spirits came out of a fire and danced about on the bed linens. In "Sleep" (1816) ghosts played on the ceiling and in the author's first major work "Ruslan and Liudmila" (1820) all the fanciful aspects of a fairy tale appeared. The work is in many respects a parody of the serious spiritualism of Zhukovsky.

It is interesting that Pushkin's close friends in the lyceum did not use specters or ghosts in their poetry. Delvig, Yakovlev, Korsakov, Rzhevsky and Kuchelbecker refrained from using the supernatural. One reason might be the strict rules by which the students of the lyceum lived. They were rarely in society where perhaps literature or poetry having mystical elements would be discussed. Yet it is peculiar that such themes are not in the poetry of Pushkin's close acquaintances at the lyceum.

As Pushkin matured in the early nineteenth century, he retained a belief and an interest in the esoteric. He showed considerable concern in 1820 when a fortune teller named Kirchow read his future in cards. She told him that he would receive money, a business proposition and fame. A threat was also related. She reported that he would be deported twice and would live a long time if at the age of thirty-seven he could avoid great danger in the form of a white head, a white horse or a white man.[51] The irony of the latter is well known. The writer was killed at the age of thirty-seven in a duel with George D'Anthes.

In the early 1820s Pushkin began to use spirits and demons in an attributive sense, as an element of romantic stylization. In "The Conversation of the Bookseller with the Poet" (824), the writer admonished a bookseller for being more interested in money than in poetic inspiration. The latter was attributed to a supernatural power, a demon, which existed in poets: "A certain demon possessed my play and leisure: he flew at me everywhere. He whispered wonderful sounds to me." (32-37) The mystical nature of poetical inspiration was heightened by the symbol of the demon.

Pushkin often used dreams to tone down the supernatural and spiritualistic images in his literary works. In "The

Brigand Brothers" (1822), apparitions haunt the younger brother in a dream as the specters flaunt themselves in a dance macabre. In the short parody "The Bridegroom" (1830), ghosts appear during sleep. In "The Bridegroom" (1825), a dream is fabricated by the bride to divulge the suitor's murder of a girl in a forest hideaway. Imminent murders are seen in the dreams of Aleko in "The Gypsies" (1824); Tatiana in "Eugene Onegin," and of Maria Gavrilovna in "The Snowstorm" (1820). Mozart sees a foreboding specter of his own death in "Mozart and Salieri" (1830) and the hero of "The Captain's Daughter," Grinev, previews the general carnage of the Pugachev uprising in a dream. Pushkin also uses a dream to cover blasphemy in the Holy Mary's annunciation dream in "Gavriliada" (1820). The famous poet's stylization of dreams was a literary device that was to be used by Russian authors throughout the nineteenth century.

Pushkin's superstitious nature once saved him from possible involvement in the Decembrist Revolution. On December 11, 1825, just before the revolt in St. Petersburg, the poet was in exile at the family estate Mikhailovskoe where he is known to have had a copy of "The Interpreter of Dreams" on his desk.[52] Eager to see his friends in the city, he decided on impulse to make a dash for the capital. His superstitious forebodings stopped him from going because of the strange things that occurred during his departure: a hare crossed the road with flattened ears and outstretched paws when the writer went to tell friends goodbye; the servant who was to accompany him became ill; and he passed a priest dressed in black when the carriage finally started the journey. The poet was too apprehensive to overlook so many evil omens and returned to his estate.[53] The next day the Decembrist Revolt took place and many of the writer's acquaintances were involved. Pushkin dreamed that five of his teeth fell out and decided that it was a premonition of the death of his friends, five of whom were later hanged.[54]

Two of Pushkin's great contributions to world literature used the supernatural for dramatic effect. In the famous novel in verse *Eugene Onegin*, the heroine Tatiana's famous dream was full of ominous creatures; and the ill-fated Lenskii saw a vision before his well-known duel with Onegin. However, of all the fantastic scenes that Pushkin wrote, the most famous were in his classical romantic story *The Queen of Spades*. Part of the plot of the tale was told to the writer by the Moscow Governor-General Golitsyn, whose grandmother had lived in Paris and had given her grandson a series of winning cards.[55] He played them and won back his losses. Pushkin's creative inventiveness developed the rest of the story, which might have been told tongue-in-cheek as a parody of the spiritualistic stories so popular at the time.

The Romantic stylization of *The Queen of Spades* is unique. Studies have shown that the language of the story is close to poetry, and the Gothic and romantic images in Hermann's imagination when he thinks of the winning cards give psychological depth to the hero's characterization.[56] The supernatural ending of the story—the winking Queen of Spades—was toned down by a classic epilogue in which the fate of the personages was detailed literally and suggestively in the syntax.[57]

The sophisticated literary stylization of spiritualistic images in Pushkin's mature works indicates a significant development from the ghosts and spirits of his early literary efforts. In a way his development is a reflection of what took place in Russian literature during the early nineteenth century. The literal nature of Zhukovsky's romantic spirits changed into reasoned suggestiveness and intimation in the works of Pushkin, whose style represented the quintessence of Western spiritualism and the folk tradition. Trained in peasant lore by his nanny and imbued with Western literature in school, Pushkin's sagacity was evident in the cleverness of his stylization. The reign of Alexander ended when Russian literature was entering a period of obsession with the spiritualistic. The literature of the 1830s and 1840s displayed a tremendous popularity of the occult among the reading public, which eagerly accepted the sophisticated literary stylization developed by Pushkin.

The death of the Emperor Alexander I in 1825 adds to the mystical nature of his reign. While on a visit to Taganrog, the tsar died at the age of forty-eight. He had gone to the small town on the Sea of Azov for a visit with a royal relative who had been sent there by doctors for medical treatment. The ruler's sudden demise has been the subject of speculation ever since.[58] It has been reported that his death was actually a ruse which allowed him to abdicate and spend the remainder of his life in Siberia as a monk in search of salvation. There are, however, factors which indicate that the wary monarch did indeed pass away at Taganrog.

Alexander knew that he would have to give up his participation in governmental rule if he was to have a chance for a religious life. He made several allusions to abdication in conversations with members of his family so that he could retire and lead a quiet life somewhere on the Rhine.[59] Since there was no apparent cause for his death, it has been assumed that he carried out his dream and left the throne. Yet there are conflicting reports about his disappearance. Military officers testified to the resemblance between the late tsar and a hermit named Fedor Kuzmich in Siberia. The Earl of Cathcart was supposed to have taken the tsar to Palestine where he became a monk; and a satchel found after the death of Fedor Kuzmich revealed a note that was decoded with a message from the Emperor Paul to his wife about Alexander's being involved in a plot for his murder.[60] However, there is evidence to indicate that the tsar did pass away at Taganrog. There was a corpse and the tsar's mother Maria Fedorovna did accept the body as that of her son. Several parties, including the empress, would have had to know about the scheme if the tsar did feign death. No historical evidence has shown that any of the people who would have been involved participated in such a guise. For this study, it is interesting that the reign of the enigmatic and mystically inclined monarch should have ended in mystery.

Part III

The Reign of Nicholas I: Censorship and Anagogic Literature

Emperor Nicholas I who was known as a despot throughout most of his thirty-year reign, made a striking contrast to his mystical predecessor Tsar Alexander I. Nicholas' education, personality, and interests had little in common with that of his older brother. As the younger son of the dethroned Emperor Paul, Nicholas had developed into a family man, a defender of the Russian Orthodox Church, and a military statistician. He had no time for spiritualism in his life, nor did he have any interest in the occult sciences. Yet, amazingly, during his reign, Russian society was preoccupied with séances and mediums, and Russian literature produced its greatest romantic works. The contrast between the rise of spiritualism in society and literature with the puritanical interests of Nicholas' court is indeed unique.

Several factors are responsible for the differences between the Russian court and Russian society during Nicholas' reign. The tsar's education and devotion to the Russian church contributed to his lack of interest in philosophy and spiritualistic movements. Censorship in the 1830s and 1840s played a role in limiting the subject matter available to authors and directed their talents to subtle ways of avoiding restrictions, such as through parody and suggestive literature. Literary movements from Europe greatly influenced the writers in Russia where restraints hindered the free development of their artistic drives. Byronism from England and Hoffmanism from Germany were especially influential during this period. Literary developments and spiritualistic interests were alien to Nicholas' court, which was aloof and content.

While Nicholas I was born in the last year of his grandmother Catherine II's reign, the former Empress did not make any provisions for his education as she had done with his older brothers Alexander and Constantine. Nicholas' doting mother and father, the Emperor Paul, directed his training from the cradle on. The Empress Marie was an example of public and private virtues. She surrounded her son with women tutors: a Miss Lyon who was Scottish;[1] Julie Adlerbert, an English widow; and Madame de Lieven who was Westphalian. Tsar Paul was captivated by military strategy and parades. His son was reared to be a soldier and was given his first military uniform at the age of three.[2] With the religious influence from his mother and the military life from his father, Nicholas had no time for developing more sophisticated interests or for studying subjects that would have broadened his mind. He grew up a military statistician and the defender of the Russian Orthodox Church.

The nature of the Russian church could have encouraged the spread of the interest in the occult in Russia. There was much mysticism in the church services. People stood in awe of a ceremony which was performed by beautifully robed and bearded priests speaking in Old Church Slavonic which the average Russian could not understand. Prince Adam Czartoryski gave the following description of a ceremony in his memoirs: “The Russian rite reminds one rather of pagan than of Christian observances. The bishops and priests, all with long beards, involuntarily recall to one’s mind the high priests of antiquity. Everything is calculated for pomp and an appeal to the senses. There is no provision for that religion of the heart, lifting up the soul to the Creator which demands tranquility and reflection.”[3] It is possible that spiritualism satisfied elements of the public’s spiritual and intellectual needs which the rigid and dogmatic Russian church could not gratify.

In the article “Something about Specters,” the noted poet V.A. Zhukovsky discussed society’s interests in specters in 1848 as if the question of spiritualistic phenomena was a major concern of the time. The writer’s observations indicate that considerable thought was spent on the fascination with spirits and specters among the Russian public. Zhukovsky wrote:[4] “Should one believe or not believe in specters? Before one can answer this question, one must define what a specter is:

1. ‘I saw’ means with my open eyes, wide awake, a subject formed so that it was acceptable to the sense of sight.
2. ‘I dreamed’ means I saw with closed eyes and not in full reality a subject that did not belong to the sense of sight.
3. ‘I imagined’ means I saw, wide awake, with open eyes, a subject not belonging to reality.”[4]

And so, a specter is a materialization of a non-material object. If this object which seems to us real and which is separate from us at the moment we see it, is nothing else but something taking place inside our organ of sight, then it has no existence in itself. In such an occurrence there is no specter. Such a thing occurs, then, when a spiritual substance forms before us which is seen by us and does not belong to the realm of sight. Consequently, to believe or not believe in specters means should one believe in the actuality of such substances and their communication with us through the senses?

When we sleep, all other actions cease to act on us, and seeing a dream, we see without a subject while not using the sense of sight. If dreams were not so common, it only a few had them, and if they had them rarely, then dreams would seem rather implausible, or they would seem rather contradictory to natural processes. Yet dreams which are completely similar to what we call specters occur while one is wide awake. Sometimes the eyes have not closed and surrounding objects are still seen by us, but already a dream has taken over us and in the dream we have already gone into something without sensing it which forms something that is completely different from what we were thinking of at the moment. It is something strange that always more or less causes us to sense horror; and if we awaken, not having noticed our quick transference from vigilance to sleep and back again, then it is easy to assume that nothing unnatural occurred. The late A.M. Druzhinin, a former head of a Moscow teaching institution told me the following remarkable tale:

> I was (as he told me) briefly acquainted with a Dr. Berkovich. Once in the winter he invited me along with a Mrs. Perets to an evening party. We spent the evening completely happy and the host was espe-

cially joyful. At ten o'clock the wife of the doctor said to him, "Go and see if they've set the table. It's time to eat." A door from the living room led directly into the dining room. Berkovich left and returned in a minute. "Soon?" his wife asked. He silently nodded. I looked at him and saw that he was pale as linen. His gaiety ceased and the rest of the evening he hardly said a word. We sat at the table and ate. Mrs. Perets decided to leave and Dr. Berkovich conducted his guest outside. Seating her in her carriage, he fell on his knees in the snow which lay in heaps around the entranceway. (There had been a horrible snowstorm all day.) Evidently he caught a cold at that moment. The next day they came to me and told me that Berkovich was ill in bed and was asking for me. I myself had wanted an early visit with him because the morose gloominess he had shown bothered me. And when I asked him about his behavior he answered, "I shall soon die. I saw with my own eyes my own death. When I left the room yesterday evening I went to the dining room to inquire about the table. I saw a casket on the table surrounded by candles and that I myself was lying in it. You can be sure that you will soon bury me." And actually, Berkovich did die in a short time.

It is entirely possible that there was a disease in embryo in his body at the time, that the cold developed the disease, and that the disease with the help of his imagination, frightened by the specter, led to his death. But what was the specter? A dream while awake or a vision of a form that doesn't exist, like those that occur when a feverous condition of the soul or an upset and ill body causes a dream-like

> state. In this case, there was nothing which is derived from the same cause that produced any sort of vision. Here the vision is not separated from the one who is seeing it, a vision without a subject; here there is still no specter in the sense as we defined it, while there is in actuality something unusual and not belonging to the natural order of things.

Zhukovsky also related a tale told to him by the poet N.N. Marav'ev, who, the author mentioned, was not at all superstitious:

> Once I studied in Gottingen. An English student named Stewart was very funny and we teased him a lot. Once he bragged that nothing would frighten him and I made a bet with him and won. He swore revenge because he was offended, but soon after he left the university. Time passed. Once in the middle of the night I awoke and glanced around my room. Stewart was sitting in an armchair. I told him to leave but his dark eyes stared at me. I continued to shout abuses at him for bothering me at such a late hour, but he didn't move. Finally I realized that it was a specter and I ran my saber through it. Nothing happened. It simply sat and stared. Toward morning it went through the locked door and disappeared. I never heard of Stewart or saw the apparition again. [5]

In concluding his article about specters, Zhukovsky turned to the religious aspects of the issue: "All forms of specters relate to one question: should one believe or not believe in specters? A majority of occurrences seem evidence enough to cause us to answer the question positively; on the other hand, the unbelievable nature of the same occurrences which departs from the usual order of things, inclines us to answer negatively. Which answer should we select? Neither one nor the other. While almost all proof used for the reality of specters has as much strength as the historical proof used as the basis of many events in ages past which we accept for the truth, and while there is no reason to accept as impossible that which we can't explain, these phenomena will still always remain between "yes" and "no" for us. The Creator put a secret curtain between us and the other world. This curtain is impenetrable . . . Therefore, not denying either the existence of sprits or the possibility of their communication with us . . . we shall not dare or wish to open their fatal message. It could destroy our faith."[6]

Zhukovsky, the romantic poet who introduced ghosts and vampires to Russian poetry, preferred to leave the question of specters unanswered. Expressing a different attitude than he did when he presented spirits quite literally in his poetry at the beginning of the century, the mature writer showed society's concern and confusion over the interest in spiritualism. Communication with spirits had no place in the dogma of the Russian Orthodox Church and the problem of how to accept it in relationship with the church was undoubtedly a matter of intellectual concern for many at the time. The religious question was discussed by Prince Adeka in a letter addressed to the "Revue Spirits" in Paris: "Spiritualism as a doctrine was introduced into Russia in 1854 by M. Boltine and some others who had witnessed spiritual phenomena abroad and had become acquainted with the works of Allan Kardec . . . Unhappily, however,

Russia not yet being with a free press, the advocates of spiritualism have had to keep in the background with the public. The State Church does not allow the publication, in the Russian language, of any books, pamphlets, or printed matter discussing it: it is therefore only a subject of private discussion among those who know other languages.

"Russia has a penal code in which any Russian who steps outside the pale of the Greco-Russian church, or who attempts to teach doctrines contrary to it, is punishable by exile to Siberia. Such is the legal situation of the various sects in Russia. Happily, however, laws there are laxly observed. The dogmas of the State Church are by the mass of the people assented to chiefly as a means of keeping themselves clear of the police. But very many, as opportunity comes, throw aside the mask and join some sect; and sects in Russia are numerous.

"Spiritualists in Petersburg are necessarily of the educated classes only. Many . . . go to séances as to an entertainment. There are also many others to whom it is a demonstrated science. They study its doctrines and practice its morality. My remarks have had reference to spiritualism as it is in the capital, but there is plenty of evidence that it is studied all through the provinces."[7]

The prince's letter indicates the problems early spiritualists had in expressing their views in public and perhaps explains why Zhukovsky's article was so guarded in its conclusions.

Zhukovsky was not the only major author who was writing about psychic phenomena during the 1840s and 1850s. The greatest authors of the nineteenth century were also attending séances and investigating the communication of spirits that was causing so much concern. I.S. Turgenev, L.N. Tolstoy, and F.M. Dostoevsky attended séances during that time and their reports on the mediumistic activities they observed will be presented later. For now, it is important to understand the developments in Russian literature during Nicholas I's reign to appreciate how Russian letters both reflected the phenomenon of spiritualism and contributed to its spread.

There was more "second worldliness" in the Russian mystical tales of the nineteenth century than in the fanciful stories of the eighteenth. Authors wrote on the assumption that there existed another inaccessible sensitivity and incomprehensible spiritual world. This second "other" world had secretive and even harmful influences on man. In the religious sense, the otherworldliness was a reflection of the philosophy of Schelling, which had tremendous influence on Western and Russian literature at the beginning of the nineteenth century.[8]

Two strong Western literary currents, Byronism and Hoffmanism, were influential in the Russian literary scene from the 1820s into the 1850s. Both had a romantic basis and their appeal to Russian writers of this period was due to certain political and social developments in the country. Literary censorship by the government had narrowed the writer's world. The censorship law of 1826, a voluminous enactment of 230 articles, charged the censors to direct public opinion according to "the existing conditions and views of the government."[9] The harmful measure was an overreaction to the Decembrist Revolution of 1825, and it began the extremely severe censorship measures of the next thirty years. The multiplicity of agencies with the sanctioned power to exercise censorship was phenomenal. Practically every governmental department could exercise restrictions on literature, including the post office and the department of horse breeding.[10] Writers dared not express openly their political and social views if they were negative in nature. Parody became a means of escape. The fancifulness of Hoffman's romantic style gave Russian writers such as Gogol a vehicle for political and social satire. The disdainfulness of Byronism appealed to Lermontov who saw the Russian gentleman of the upper class in a role similar to that of the Byronic hero. Writers also turned to history as a means of escaping censors and romantic parody and literary stylization appeared in a series of historical novels. It was remarkable that there was such an outpouring of literature in a period so oppressed by censorship. Yet it was the specter-filled literature of the 1830s and 1840s that could have given direction to the public's social and spiritualistic needs. Many young people were directed toward social upheaval by the disillusionment promoted by Byronism. The discontent in Russian universities during the later 1850s and early 1860s could have been encouraged by the dissatisfaction produced in the earlier literature. Spiritually, young people were disheartened and the fantastic world of the earlier literature could have directed some to spiritualism which was so popular in Western countries during the period. The otherworldliness of Hoffmann's tales and the Byronic confrontation with fate gave the Russian readers a taste for the unknown and encouraged the spread of spiritualism in the 1850s.

The fantastic and spiritualistic elements in Hoffmann's stories appealed to the Russian reading public because of the mysticism being discussed and reported in society. For instance, A.S. Pushkin wrote in his diary on December 17, 1833 the following: "They're speaking about a strange occurrence in town. In one of the homes belonging to the directors of the court stables, furniture took it upon itself to move and jump about; the affair went to the authorities.

Prince V. Dolgorukii is in charge of the investigation. One of the clerks called in a priest, but during the prayers, the chairs and table did not want to stand still. Various interpretations are going about."[11]

This incident was also mentioned by P.A. Viazemsky in a letter to A.I. Turgenev and also by A. I. Bulgakov in a letter.[12] The latter correspondent who served as Postmaster General I Moscow during the 1830s and 40s and who was known for his correspondence mentioned several strange incidents in his years of communication by pen with his friends. For instance, on January 17, 1821, Bulgakov reported the following: "The youngest of the Shakhovsky countesses was subject to nervous attacks. (I am referring to the family of Alexander Mikhailovich who was then dead. He had eight daughters). Dr. Lebental magnetized her. He had just put her to sleep when she said some words in a somnambulistic state, which no one could understand. Later when her mother asked, 'What did you say?' She answered, 'A prayer.' 'In what language?' 'In Latin.' Yet she did not know that language. Her mother laughed, but the daughter took a pen and wrote the whole prayer in Latin. The mother said that what she had written was just nonsense, but the patient immediately translated the prayer into French. When the doctor arrived, the countess gave him the Latin prayer to read. 'Is this familiar to you?' 'No, but it is a prayer.' 'Has she written it well?' 'Very well, and with no errors.' 'Read this.' 'This is a translation of the Latin prayer.' All of this sounds supernatural to me. I am sending you the prayer and the translation. If anyone but the Countess Shakhovsky had told me, I'd think that the doctor was in cahoots with her . . . (also) the young countess talks in her sleep to say what medicine she should be given and gives the proportions in Latin, even ounces."[13]

In another letter February 8, 1827, Bulgakov reported the visions that his acquaintance S. S. Apraksin had experienced.[14] Such incidents were popular in the gossipy salons of the early nineteenth century and no doubt encouraged the interest in supernatural literature.

A decisive turn toward prose literature occurred among the Russian reading public during the latter 1820s. The trend has been traced to Zhukovsky's early prose-ballad "The Red Carbuncle" in 1816.[15] The influx of foreign translations during the period also helped contribute to the demand for prose. The first translation of a story by Hoffmann was in 1822 when "Das Fraulein von Scudery" was printed in the "Son of the Fatherland," a journal started by N.I. Grech in 1812 for war propaganda and later changed into a literary work.[16] Hoffmann's short stories consisted of three major sets of tales: "Fantasiestucke in Callots Manier" (1815), "Die Nachtstucke" (1817), and "Die Serapionsbruder" (1921). In 1823 the writer's "Doge and Dogaresse" was also printed in the journal mentioned above and by1829 there was a Hoffman craze in Russia.

A.P. Pogorelsky

The first Russian write to emulate the famous German writer of tales was Pogorelsky (the pen name for A.V. Perovsky). In 1825 the sophisticated Russian writer published in *The News of Literature* a story entitled "The Poppy-seed Cake Seller of the Lafertovskii Slum." It was the first truly fantastic prose work in Russian fiction. There was no explanation given for the incredible intervention of evil powers in the lives of the inhabitants.[17] The story was told in a very light style with humorous touches, but caused consternation among critics because the cat that changed into human form did so without revealing the manner of its feat. The editor of *The News of Literature*, A.E. Voiekov wrote that the heroine must have imagined that the cat became human.[18] Russians were used to specters in their poetry, but they were not yet prepared for the esoteric in their prose. Pushkin even wrote in 1827 in a poem to E.N. Ushakova: "in our days there are a lot less devils and specters. God knows to where they've gone."[19] The great Russian poet was soon to create specters of his own in some of the greatest Russian prose works. The reading public's attitudes changed quickly and by the 1830s specters and apparitions abounded in literature.

In 1828 Pogorelsky included the tale of the poppy-seed cake seller in a book, *My Evenings in Little Russia: or the Double*."[20] The author and his double related many stories about apparitions, doubting their verisimilitude and discussing their historical origins. The work consists of six evenings of discussions. Skulls, visions, magicians and sorcerers dominate. The sixth evening is a *coup de maitre:* a tale about a man who was reared by apes on the island of Borneo. Colonel van der K. was lost as a child on the island and was adopted by a large ape name Tutu. Needless to say, his situation preceded Tarzan's by many years.

In 1829 Pogorelsky followed his novel with a moralistic fairy tale entitled "The Black Hen, or Underground Inhabitants," which was published in *Magic Stories for Children*.[21] The story became very popular and A.S. Pushkin said that he read it through twice without stopping. The notoriety Pogorelsky received led to his acceptance in a literary circle including Baron Delvig, Pushkin and other writers. He became a contributor to *The Literary Gazette*.[22] In that periodical, the writer's novel *The Convent Girl* began appearing with the final part published in 1833.

Pogorelsky blended the supernatural with an adventure tale in the work that preceded the historical novels of the 1830s. The novel is an exciting, fast-moving melodrama that received favorable critical response. It was called one of the earliest and best of the works of the "ethnographical school" which prepared the way for Gogol's tales in the 1830s.[23]

After Pogorelsky's poppy-seed story, the next fantastic tale to appear in Russian journals was "The Secluded House," published in *Northern Flowers* in 1829.[24] The story was long thought to have been written by V.P. Tito (Titan Kosmokratov) under whose name it was published, but the story about an evil spirit that rode a cart about Vasilevskii Island was later revealed to be a creation of Pushkin's. In the memoirs of A.P. Kern there is the mentioning of an evening when someone named Titov wrote down a story that Pushkin made up for his friend's entertainment.[25] It was later disclosed that Titov took the story to Pushkin so that he could polish the details. Pushkin's friend A. A. Delvig encourage Titov to publish the work because spiritualistic stories had become a favorite of the reading public.[26]

The popularity of specters and esoteric creatures in literature by the 18320s can be seen in an introduction written by O.M. Somov for his story "The Werewolf" (1829): "Am I guilty that my indefatigable contemporary romantic writers have used up all fanciful titles: Corsairs, specters . . . and even vampires have made inroads on the reading generation or have hidden themselves in the moonlight in the boudoirs of sensitive girls. My imagination is so full of all these live and dead horrors, I myself even, although as a joke, have decided to scare you. I shall only say in justification of my title that I wanted to make a gift to you of something new, not done before; and Russian werewolves, as such as I remember, have not scared good people in literary scenes.[27]

Somov's turn to fantastic subjects was a departure from his earlier literary works. His novel *Gaidamak* (1827) had only one element of the supernatural: the hero tells a legend about a dishonest man. During the man's death a fiery pillar appeared over his home and burned the edifice. Later the dead man was seen being carried through the village in his coach by dead servants. The hero's recounting of the legend accentuates his own character and adds atmosphere to the literary work. The use of Ukrainian folk legends as a literary device became one of the basic traits of Somov's literary style.

Specters, werewolves and apparitions became so common in Russian literature in the early 1830s they soon formed the basis for parody. Continuing the line of writers influenced by Hoffmann, O.I. Senkovsky wrote a number of fanciful works which used parody in a Hoffmannesque style to criticize elements of society. In "The Fantastic Travels of Baron Drambeisa" (1833)[28], readers are chastised for never reading prefaces, so a preface is inserted in the first section of the work to fool the unwary reader. In "The Notes of a House-spirit" (1835), the author criticized journalists and belittled the sanctity of marriage. In "The Transformation of Heads into Books and Books into Heads" (1839), the uneducated public is again rebuked. Senkovsky's most amusing parody was "A Large Outing at Satan's" which criticized several aspects of society and literature. At the outing where Satan is interviewing his flock of devils, the evil-spirit of romanticism explained a personal problem to his chief as follows: "Alas, how I've suffered. A woeful dampness has penetrated to the walls of my soul . . . I have been chased into a murderous cave of terror and stench, full of rotting corpses and laughing skeletons."

"What does this mean?" asked a stunned Satan.

"It means I have a head cold," Romanticism answered.

During the 1830s spirits were discussed, believed and parodied. Later in the middle of the century in the novel *Oblomov*, the writer I.A. Goncharov pictured the interest of country landowners in dreams and superstitions.[31] The Hoffmann craze heightened the interest in psychic phenomena and perhaps no author was more greatly influenced by the times and by Hoffman than a remarkable writer from the Ukraine, Gogol.

N.V. Gogol

Knowing the public's zest for the esoteric, Gogol wrote highly stylized stories in a Hoffmannesque manner about the legends of spirits and witches in the Ukraine.[32] When he ran out of material, he wrote to his mother and urged her to send him more oddities about Ukrainian beliefs and legends.[33] He had read Hoffman in German and in French translations before the writer had become popular in Russia. The similarities of Gogol's and Hoffmann's stylization of the fantastic are evident: for instance, the treatment of the supernatural in the German's story *The King's Bride* and the Russian's masterpiece *Dead Souls*. The former is a satirical tale about distorted human beings and dwarfish creatures. It is concerned with the follies and vices of man as well as the writer's role in society. The latter is known for its human caricatures and one of its major themes is the burden of the writer in society. However, the unique similarity of the two works is the authors' manner of expression.

1. Both authors distort human movements in a similar way:

> In *The King's Bride*, chapter three, he writes, "Baron Porphyrio von Ockerodastes . . . threw himself in the air . . . while his feet beat trochees, and pyrrhics."
>
> In *Dead Souls*, chapter two, Gogol writes, "Chichikov covered the room in two leaps each time slapping his behind quite deftly with his heels." The in chapter three he says, "Chichikov put on his suspenders . . . and performed a caper."
>
> The heroes of the two works are not the only ones who jump about. In *The King's Bride*, chapter three, "While their retinue continued their Olympic Games butting one another in their pointed stomachs with their fat heads and turning back somersaults, flinging themselves up into the air . . ."
>
> And in *Dead Souls*, chapter six, "All the domestics were going through such leaps as even the sprightliest of male ballet dancers could hardly succeed in performing . . ."

2. Both writers utilized elements of folklore; in both works animals have human dignity and roosters quarrel over gallantry in both prose writings and things talk in each work. Carrots converse in *The King's Bride* and horses speak in *Dead Souls*. Both writers used exaggerated noises: "the laughter from the soil" of *The King's Bride* and the "strange hissing" in *Dead Souls*.

Gogol also imitated Hoffmann's stylization of the fantastic by using ridiculous delineation of objects, by talking with the reader in a theatrical manner, and by generalizing the ridiculous and the sublime. However, as with Hoffman, Gogol strove to impart social and moral lessons in his fantastically stylized prose. The two works by the authors mentioned above can also serve to illustrate this point.

Concern for the writer's role in society is a theme in both "Dead Souls" and *The King's Bride*. In chapter four of the latter the author says, "The poet's weapon is the work, the song. I can have as my foe a Tartaric battle son, I can strike him down with pointed epigrams, beat him to the ground with dithyrambs full of amorous frenzy—these are the weapons of the true poet."

Gogol also wrote about the attacks that writers face from a society that was his foe as well as his friend. In the beginning of chapter three of *Dead Souls*, there is a lengthy discussion of the fate of the poet. The writer's struggle is also a topic in chapters eight and eleven. Of course, the plight of an author was a popular theme in nineteenth century literature and is only one of many themes in Gogol's novel.

Gogol and Hoffman were both concerned with human folly and vice. However, in *Dead Souls* there is no means of enhancing his social and financial position. The one suggestive line in the book is a joke. In chapter ten the chairman of the administrative offices asks Korobochka if the buyer of souls "tried to seduce her." Gogol's laugh is heard here; but he showed more than he realized. When he does suggest the physical, he must do so in jest. It is unique that an author who wished to display the vices of mankind left out the most popular: pride, wrath, envy, gluttony, avarice and sloth are common vices in *Dead Souls*, but there is no lust. But what is perhaps even more unusual is that the author's exaggerated notion of the work's significance indicated that he did not realize that he had omitted one of the more common vices. Instead he created a comic masterpiece; and evidence indicates that Hoffmann's manner of stylization of the fantastic helped Gogol produce his great literary contribution.

Gogol's concern with social issues in his fanciful works was investigated by D.S. Merezhkovsky in his book *The Fate of Gogol* (1903).[34] The critic stated that Gogol was actually interested in defeating the bureaucracy through the literary medium.[35] The writer who used devils and evil spirits in a whimsical manner was in a Holy War to save Russia from the bureaucratic morass that writers since Pushkin had attacked.[36]

Gogol's moralistic and fantastic stories began in 1821 when his "Evenings on a Farm near Dikanka" were pulished.[37] Every story contains spirits and devils and the writer also introduced exorcism to Russian literature. In the tale "St. John's Eve," a priest tries to exorcise a village that had been bothered by the devil. In "The Lost Letter," the devils had pig faces and a bewitched horse flew through the air. Another exorcism was tried in the story "A Terrible Vengeance," but the priest was not able to force the evil spirit from the possessed victim's body. In his "Confessions," Gogol mentions how he contrived the unusual scenes he pictured in his literature: "Suffering from fits of despair, the origin of which I could scarcely explain to myself . . . I used to imagine the most ridiculous scenes, picture to myself absurd personages and characters, and place them in circumstances as ridiculous as themselves."

Gogol imagined the unimaginable and most of his famous prose works end with a symbolic apparition: the hovering "Overcoat" in which he criticized Russian bureaucracy;

the mysterious troika in *Dead Souls*, which heralded Russia as the savior of mankind; and the lamp-lighting devil in *Nevskii Prospect* which proclaimed that evil exists in the world. Gogol's obsession with spirits was probably a result of the time, but he wrote like a medieval moralist. His religiosity and secluded life allowed him to accept the unreal; since evil spirits existed in his religion, why then couldn't apparitions exist in reality? The great number of specters in his works suggests that they were more than just a matter of romantic stylization, that they were actually believed by the artist. Whatever the nature of his spirits, Gogol's literary creations could certainly have contributed to the public's fascination with spiritualism.

Another literary influence that could have encouraged the spread of spiritualism, but to a small degree, was Byronism. The Byronic hero disdained his existence and sought another, better world. His search for the unknown was similar to the quest of the spiritualist who sought contact and knowledge of another world. Byronism was joined with Hoffmanism in a book in 1833 when N.A. Polevoi wrote *The Felicity of Madness*, which presented a Byronic hero in a story with Hoffmannesque stylization. The book was based on a German story, "Meister Flog," but the novel was a weak imitation of the tale and did not bring the author fame.[39] Polevoi's book is important only because it blended two romantic literary attitudes which related to the esoteric. Byronism was promulgated during this period by a far more important and talented writer: Lermontov.

M. I. Lermontov

In 1840 Lermontov finished his prose masterpiece, *A Hero of Our Time*. The hero of the book, Pechorin, was a young man with many Byronic traits. The work was very successful and young men in Russian society patterned themselves after the hero, creating a generation of disillusioned upper-class men. In the section of the novel called "The Fatalist," Pechorin mentioned his own weariness of life: "In the vain battle of existence, I exhausted both the ardor of my soul and the constancy of my will . . . I became bored and dissolute."

His sentiments were a repetition of the plight of Byron's famous heroes: "He would find a life within itself, to breathe without mankind." ("Childe Harold," canto three, stanza twelve) "There was in him a vital scorn of all." ("Lara," canto one, stanza eighteen) "He hated man too much to feel remorse." ("The Corsair," stanza eleven) "I disdained to mingle with the herd." ("Manfred," Act III, Scene I)

To escape the dissolute world, Pechorin turned to the road: "My life became emptier day after day, there remained for me only one means of escape, travel!" (Princess Mary) The Byronic heroes also turned to travel. Don Juan, the Giaour, Lara, Manfred and others were on the move and not one found contentment.

With such figures as heroes, no wonder the Russian gentlemen of the middle nineteenth century became despondent. Many forces were affecting them: the awakening social consciousness in the country which preached that serfdom, the economic basis of the landed gentry for hundreds of years, was a deplorable system; and the Russian social structure forbade professions for the upper class outside of those found acceptable in the rigid system itself: military, civil service or estate management. Nineteenth-century social mores created a desire for a way out of the social dilemma. Spiritualism appealed to many who wished to escape such a world.

Lermontov's Byronism might have played a minor role in the spread of spiritualism in the 1850s, but the writer himself was never greatly interested in the occult. He did write a play, "The Masquerade," based on a mystery in his family history. His grandfather, M.B. Arsen'ev, poisoned himself in 1810 while waiting in his costume as the jailer in "Hamlet." The play was to be given on his estate and a neighboring countess was supposed to attend. After she did not appear, the body of Lermontov's grandfather was found. The circumstances of the death and the reasons for it were never cleared up, but the author's grandmother did not attend her husband's funeral.

Two poems with devilish demons by Lermontov indicate the author's knowledge of the occult. His most famous poem with supernatural elements is "The Demon," which was not published during his lifetime.[41] As many as eight versions of the work dating from 1829 to 1841 were circulated widely through Russian society. The fatalistic cynicism of the poem caused the censors to reject its publication. The humane disillusioned Demon sought salvation through love, but the necessity of evil in a world crated by an all good, all-powerful God is a truth stronger than the creature's desire and tragic despair. Lermontov changed the nature of his demon in the poem "A Tale for Children." The devil is a corrupt dandy of the 1840s who came to St. Petersburg to prey on the heroine. Social criticism is evident in this second demonic poem by the poet's reference to the "dirty walls of palaces and alums" where deceit, madness, and suffering exist.

A spirit with heavenly qualities is in the poet's work "The Angel" (1931)[42] but aside from angels and demons, Lermontov might have had the new science of spiritualism in mind when he wrote his poem "The Dream," which was not published in his lifetime. A wounded soldier on a field in Dghestan drifts into deathly slumber thinking about his beloved, who is waiting for him where flowers are blooming and pleasant conversations are taking place. Later the heroine dreams of a body on the sands of a valley. The transmigration of the human spirit was a familiar topic among spiritualists and Lermontov wrote "The Dream" in 1841, a time when he was interested enough in spirits to write a parody about them, "Shtoss."

Lermontov's presentation of "Shtoss" to the public was as strange as the story itself. In 1841 he invited several acquaintances together for a "four hour reading of his latest novel:"[43] "He demanded that we should foregather early in the evening and that the doors should be locked to keep out strangers. We complied with everything he wished and a select group of about thirty gathered. At last Lermontov came into the room carrying a huge notebook under his arm. A lamp was brought, the doors locked and he began reading. A quarter of an hour later he finished. The incorrigible joker had tricked us with a terrible story he had begun only the day before."

"Shtoss" was full of Gothic horrors and unlike anything Lermontov had writer before: ghosts appeared, mysteries abounded and a strange card game was played. Various interpretations of the story have been given, and the story is probably a parody of Pushkin's "Queen of Spades." Both stories started at an evening party. In Pushkin's tale, the party was at the home of a guard's officer; in Lermontov's, one guard officer was at a party. Both heroes were led to a particular house by an ominous force: Hermann went to the countess's and Lugin to Shtoss'. Both heroes entered a Rococo room and confronted two portraits. They both saw a picture of a forty-year-old man in an elegant costume and a picture of a young woman. Both heroes were possessed with a mystical card game in which the seven was very important: Herman won with the seven, but Lugin lost. A ghost came to both heroes: the old countess approached Hermann to tell him a secret about the card game and an old man visited Lugin to play cards. Hermann went mad at the end of the story, whereas Lugin mentioned at the beginning of the tale that he was going mad. Lermontov reversed aspect of Pushkin's work for humorous effect.

In a sense "Shtoss" is a parody on Lermontov's own life. Lugin, the hero of the tale, could never love without restraint, which was also true of the author.[44] When the fictional hero talked about a former love he sometimes took pleasure in making cry, one is reminded of Lermontov's youth and his treatment of young women, for instance, his love for Sofia Vielgorskaia. V.A. Sologub, a friend of the poet and a rival for Sofia's hand, married the girl after an affair full of court intrigues. Sologub later wrote that Lermontov could not really love a woman.[45] It is also curious that the musical evening at the beginning of "Shtoss" was originally written as having taken place at "Cants . . .'s" for Sologub, instead of at "Count V . . .'s" for Vielgorskaia.[46] Even the title of the story is related to the poet's life. A woman by the name of Shtoss won a large sum of money in a St. Petersburg lottery and all society was talking about her and about the chance of fate.[47] The theme of fate was linked to the word "Shtoss" and that could be the reason Lugin became afraid every time the word was mentioned.

In 1897 an ending was written for the story "Shtoss" under the pseudonym "Prince Indostanskii."[48] The tale was told as a true supernatural story. However, Lermontov himself probably did not finish the work because he was writing a parody and lost interest once he had played his joke on his friends at the evening party.

Lermontov was not the only major write to write parodies of the specter-bound literature of the time. In the 1850s, the journalist and critic A.V. Druzhinin wrote a series of humorous feuiletons which made fun of many aspects of Russian life from censorship to spiritualism. Several co-workers on the journal, such as I.I. Panaev, M.N. Longinov and others are supposed to have contributed to the book created with the amusing parodies published under the name, "The Sentimental Journey of Ivan Blackbook through Petersburg Country Homes."[49] In chapter two of the book, Mr. Blackbook explained why he had started the journey. He had been interested in black magic, but decided to give it up for love until a most dreadful experience occurred:

> "One night he was awakened by a fantastic creature that held a magic wand in its hands while its head seemed to be made of burning coals. It asked, 'Do you search for love?'
> 'Yes,' he answered the monstrous vision.
> 'Then go to the country houses.'
> 'Which ones?' Blackbook asked, inquisitive and calm.
> 'Go to the country houses!' the specter repeated."

After the third night's repetition of the command, Mr. Blackbook decided to go visiting country houses. While at the estate of the Baroness Vera (chapter eighteen) a séance was held in which it was suggested that Mr. Blackbook himself had magnetic power in his eyes, but that was soon proven to be a hoax. Druzhinin and his fellow writers laughed at the seriousness with which society accepted spiritualism, but the journalist himself was very interested in the occult. His studies of English novels of fantasy were issued during the 1850s and 60s in *The Contemporary*. Some of his comments defended writers of spiritualistic tales and discussed man's curiosity of the occult, for instance:[50] "In spite of our love for the eccentric Hoffmann, for our respect of Germans and French for their labors in the area of terror and the secret powers of nature, we must admit that a monopoly of horror stories remains with the English, or even maybe with the Americans. It may seem strange to say that people of Anglo-Saxon background, people to such a degree positive and practical, should be the outstanding fanciers . . . But moral bravery is needed for an open excursion into the strange world of the human heart. Man loves ghosts, nightmares, bloody legends; and loving them, he is certain that no one will deny him them. He tells very well the nonsense which created shivers and does not think that he has to hide his talents. That is why, if he is romantic, his talent travels along any road of fantasy; and he does not turn pale from the ridicule of critics or from the smiles of doubt from his friends."

Another writer who began writing when there was an "intellectual inclination and love for the marvelous and fantastic"[51] was Prince V.F. Odoevsky who used specters to accentuate his philosophical convictions in stories that "move easily from a recognizable setting to a mystical and sometimes aberrational realm."[52] Schelling's philosophy is evident in his tales which are concerned with the "role of the poet" and the "essence of truth."[53] His most noted work, "Russian Nights," (1844) has philosophical discussions between madness, mercantilism, logic, atheism, and the meaning of life. The writer's fantastic stories were popular in the 1830s and 40s. His "Motley Stories" (1839) were united by a literary character, Iriney Modestovich Gomozelkov, who served as a narrator for the tales.

Specters and apparitions also entered a long series of historical novels during the 1830s; however, in these works the psychic phenomena were more a matter of romantic stylization than of literal presentation of the esoteric. Writers such as M.N. Zagoshkin, A. Bestuzhev-Marlinsy, I.I. Lazhechnilov, and A.F. Weltman wrote patriotic, imaginative and sentimental historical novels with specters for dramatic effect.

The reign of Nicholas I was a period of contrasts. The tsar broke away from the folk culture and spiritualistic tradition that had started in the Russian past. The monarch's conservative court was aloof and remote from the literary and social phenomena developing around it. Schools had greatly increased the size of the Russian reading public and foreign literature such as Hoffman's and Byron's had increased the public's taste for the esoteric. Specters abounded in Russian letters and spiritualism spread among Russian society during the rule of the tsar "who had a horror of mysticism, who did not understand it and who was afraid of it."[54] The distance between the ruler and the intellectuals can be measured in his relationship with the poet Pushkin. Allowed to return from an exile that had been imposed on him for his liberal opinion, Pushkin was greatly satisfied to find out that the tsar himself would be the writer's personal censor. Yet the monarch's bias and ignorance of the author's strivings and goals soon caused friction between the two giants. Pushkin was followed continually by the police and their reports pictured the poet as a decadent. When the writer submitted his tragedy *Boris Godunov*, the tsar did not read it and sent the author a note saying that he should transform the "comedy into a historical novel in the style of Walter Scott." The absurdity of the ruler's comment offended the sensitive poet. Later a report on education in Russia, which the tsar had asked Pushkin to write, was branded as "dangerous to public security." The misunderstandings between the emperor and his subject showed the vast differences between the ruler and the intellectual movements of his time. The occult became tremendously popular during the reign of the next tsar, Alexander II, and the Russian literature and social developments of Nicholas I's rule helped create the occult's popularity.

Part IV

The Reign of Alexander II: The Occult in the Winter Palace

The reign of Alexander II, noted for the rise of evolutionary and socialistic thought in Russia, was also a period of widespread curiosity about spiritualism and the occult. The tsar, unlike his father Nicholas I, was fascinated by spiritualism and had séances conducted in the Winter Palace.[1] It is curious that the son of the famous autocrat Nicholas who loathed mysticism should have been a devotee of something as esoteric as spiritualism. Such an interest could have been developed in his youth. The future tsar's education was for the most part under the guidance of none other than V.A. Zhukovsky,[2] the romantic poet who introduced vampires in Russian literature and who wrote the treatise on specters discussed in the preceding chapter. The tsarevich grew up more a romantic than a militarist like his father. Soldiers paraded in the child's nursery wall paper and they marched in the halls and squares of the imperial capital, but the future tsar became indifferent the pomp of the military. In his travels through Russia with the famous poet as his companion, the impressionable future ruler became sympathetic toward the serfs, prisoners and other unfortunates he chanced to see in the broad Russian expanses.[3] The soft-hearted young man longed to help and understand them. He also sensed the soul of his beloved country in the songs and superstitious tales of the regions he visited. Again the folk culture tradition influenced a future monarch. The teacher also trained his pupil in the history of Karamzin "who saw a moral in every event and a visitation of Providence in every catastrophe."[4] Alexander became very religious, seeing divine guidance in his prayers. With his compassion and devotion to God, he was attracted to mediums and spiritual séances as a means of communication with divine powers. Again the folk tradition was combined with Western spiritualism and the occult science flourished during Alexander's reign.

The Tsarevich Alexander married the beautiful Wilhimina Marie of Hesse in 1841 and she became known in Russia as Maria Alexandrovna.[5] The marriage was a result of love, not political maneuvering, and the young couple shared many interests, including spiritualism. Alexander's younger brother, the Grand Duke Constantine, who would have liked to have been the heir to the throne, and who was more like their father in his militaristic interests, [6] also participated in séances with his royal brother and his family. An account of a séance left by Miss A.F. Tiutchev, a lady-in-waiting to the empress and the daughter of the famous poet F.I. Tiutchev, indicated the royal family's participation in séances. A typical gathering in the Winter Palace was made up of several aristocratic personages. Miss Tiutchev's account gave considerable insight into the happenings during a royal séance:[7] "We were all seated around a round table with our hands on the top; the warlock sat between the Empress and the Grand

Duke Constantine. Soon sounds made by spirits began to rise from the corners of the room. Questions were asked which were answered by knocks corresponding to letters of the alphabet. After a while the spirits acted weakly and revealed that there were too many people in the room and that Count Bobrinsky and I should leave. They separated us in the neighboring room from where we could hear very well what was going on in the room. The table raised about one and a half feet in the air above the floor. The Queen Mother felt as if some kind of hand touched the flounce of her dress, seized her hand and took her wedding ring. The hand remained and shook and pinched all present except the Empress, who was always avoided. It took a little bell from the hands of the sovereign and gave it to the Prince of Wurtemberg. All this aroused screams of fright and fear and surprise. I heard everything from the other room and melancholy overpowered me. I do not doubt that devils themselves were playing a bit there. I must say that the appearance of Mr. Home during the séance made a strong impression on me. Actually his face is not extraordinary: thin, feminine indefinite lines, an almost stupid appearance with nothing that would attract attention to itself, except some kind of inner fire seemed to radiate through the deathly whiteness covering his features; his eyes were open widely, staring at one point and focused with a bright shine; his mouth was half open like a man who was breathing with difficulty; and his hair began to rise and stand on his head as soon as communication with the spirits began. It seemed to form a halo of horror. Then this small little man, soft and unseen, took on the appearance of a statue or a tripod. He said that during a séance he suffers terribly. Glancing at him one wouldn't think that he was a charlatan who was trying to deceive us.

He is very taciturn, often speaking about God and religion and according to table gossip, he left the English church for Catholicism, from the point of view of orthodoxy, I believe, that the devil in essence has nothing to do with this matter since he's not interested in religious questions. The facts are too evident to argue about, and since I believe in the devil, I say that this devil wants to possess the faithful, creating for them an invisible, mystical and roughly materialized world in which it is possible to imbue the soul not by pure means but by means of various types of manipulation . . . By the way, Mr. Home and his spirits have had such enormous successes that the séance was repeated the next day at the Grand Duke Constantine's palace, Strelna; besides, there have been many séances that have passionately drawn the attention of the tsar."

Mr. Hume, the wizard that Miss Tiutchev referred to, was a Scottish spiritualist who went to Russia and achieved considerable notoriety. In England his name had been spelled Home, but in Russia the transliteration of his name was Hume. The visitor was already famous in America and Europe for his extraordinary powers. On the testimony of William Cullen Bryant and other well-known men, it is recorded that knocking on the walls, the sliding about of chairs and the levitation of the medium himself in the air occurred without the slightest recourse to trickery so far as they could observe.[8] In England his séances were attended by many prominent people, including Robert Browning and his wife. She is said to have believed in spiritualism, but he did not and was inspired to write "Mr. Sludge, the Medium" which derides Hume's practices as a hoax.[9] Charles Dickens also called Hume a "ruffian and a scoundrel."[10] Derision was also expressed in the press. In August, 1860, an editor of *Punch* exposed a "Spiritual Hume-bug" with the following poem entitled "Hume, Great Hume:"[11]

Through humbugs and fallacies though
We may roam,
Be they never so artful, there's no case like Home.
With a lift from the spirits he'll rise in the air:
(Though as lights are put out first, we can't see him
  there.)
Home, Home, Great home—there's no case like
  Home.
Of itself his accordion to play will begin
(If you don't look too hard at the works hid within)
Spirit-hands, at his bidding, will come, touch and
  go—
(But you mustn't peep under the table, you know.)

The rebuke that Hume received abroad certainly did not hinder his success in Russia. He traveled there with the celebrated novelist M. Alexandre Dumas and the medium left the following comments on his trip and his experiences after reaching the northern capital: "An amusing account of our journey may be read in Dumas' book entitled *De Paris àAstrachan*. On reaching St. Petersburg, I was honored by a kind invitation to be received by the Emperor, but which I was obliged to decline, not being in my powers at the time. His majesty most graciously sent me word that under any circumstances he would be pleased to see me. I excused myself on the plea of having so much to attend to before my marriage. A month after this, certain difficulties had arisen, and since the papers which were necessary had not appeared the marriage seemed on the point of being postponed. I had no manifestations for several months, but on this evening, I was told by the spirit of my mother to inform the Emperor the next day that my powers had returned. I did so, and was received by his majesty at the Peterhoff Palace, where I spent a week, and all the obstacles in the way of my marriage were removed by his most gracious majesty, who upon this, as upon every occasion, has shown me the greatest kindness. I have the highest veneration for him not only as a monarch, but as a man of the most kind and generous feelings."[12]

Mr. Hume also left notes on some of the happenings that occurred during his séances in Russia. The following manifestation is the medium's own description: "One evening one of my friends was converted from his previous disbelief, by seeing a hand visible to all of us in the room slowly forming in the air, a few inches above the table until it assumed the apparent materialization of a real hand visible to all of us in the room. The hand took up a pencil from the table and wrote a communication, which deeply affected the visitor who recognized it as being from his mother. The general belief is that spirit hands always appear from beneath the table, already formed, but this is incorrect for on many occasions in the presence of several persons at a time, they are seen to be formed in the manner I have described, and to melt away in the same way. Often too they have been seen to form high above our heads, and from thence to descend to the table and disappear."[13]

Whatever the cause of Mr. Hume's spirit hands, the medium certainly held his high-class audiences' attention. Prince Emil Wittgenstein, an aide-de-camp and trusted friend of the emperor, claimed that Tsar Alexander II had the most complete library of spiritual works available from the literatures of all nations.[14] The prince also wrote a letter to Mrs. Hardinge Britten, an English collector of spiritualistic phenomena, in which he described some of the problems spiritualists had in Russia and also made a reference to the monarch:[15] "The Emperor and most of his large household . . . are not only spiritualists in belief, but they would be partisans of the faith if circumstances permitted.

"Since D.D. Hume's first visit in—I think—1861, his majesty has never doubted the truth of spirit communication, and the rich presents and special favor he has bestowed on Mr. Hume, is proof positive of the royal acceptance of his medium talent.

"The great enemy of spiritualism in Russia, however, is the church. I think myself that it should be the friend of this power, for without it, the church cannot prove anything and with it, it has facts which no rival church can disprove. Perhaps you know that any writing, printing, or words spoken publicly, which offend against the articles of state religion, are punishable by the heaviest penalties—in some cases by exile to Siberia.

"Sects may arise and do, but they are offshoots if not actually a part of the church—but as for spiritualism, why, Great Heavens, it loosens the chains of ecclesiastical tyranny; breaks open the doors of the inquisition, puts out its fires, or uses them to burn the priestly passports to heaven or hell, besides making of everyone his own priest. Of course, this won't suit the ecclesiastics who live by the people's slavery, not their freedom. Hence, although spiritualism is known and believed in, alike by peer and peasant, it must be believed in, against authority—and be assured, my friend, it has a warm place in the hearts of thousands who dare not openly avow their convictions."[15]

Prince Wittgenstein's letter certainly throws light on the royal involvement in spiritualism and condemns the Russian Orthodox Church for not accepting the occult science as a part of Christian faith. His reference to Hume's success in Russia is true. Not only did the medium receive favors from the monarch, but the spiritualist married into an aristocratic family, the Kochelevs. The young couple had a child, but the wife died from tuberculosis after three years of marriage. Hume carried the disease and probably gave it to his wife.[16]

Hume's success in Russia caused a great heightening of the interest in spiritualism and one medium after another occupied the public's fancy. In 1874 M. L'vov, a great supporter of spiritualism and an aristocrat of high standing, engaged M. Bredive, a French medium, for a trip to St. Petersburg.[17] The foreigner's séances caused a sensation. One of the meetings was attended by L.N. Tolstoy and will be discussed later. Scientists were also attracted by the professor A.M. Butlerov, a noted botanist, and Professor N.N. Wagner, a distinguished zoologist, attended séances set up by the most famous Russian spiritualist of the nineteenth century, A.N. Aksakov.[18] Butlerov's detailed description of the gradual transition in his mind from skepticism to perplexity, and from perplexity to full conviction, was presented to the public in an article in the "Russian Messenger" (Russian Vestnik). "In 1871 and 18732 Mr. Hume passed some months in St. Petersburg. I have had many opportunities of being present at his séances, and all I have seen was of a nature to leave me convinced of the reality of the phenomena and of the complete absence of charlatanism on the part of Hume. I do not, of course, comprehend the manifestations in order to turn them to account for purposes of juggling or deceit. Many persons assert that these manifestations are nothing but tricks; but when the skillful conjurer Bosco conversed on the subject with Trollope, he entirely repudiated the possibility of producing by means of his art the phenomena witnessed in the presence of Hume. Carpenter, too, perceived very clearly that his "unconscious cerebration" was powerless to explain the rising of tables in the air, or the movement of objects without contact and in order to find a way out of his difficulty he simply rejected that category of phenomena, ignoring the researches of others, and not scrupling to assume that the knowledge of how to investigate without being duped belonged only to himself.

"The séances of Hume generally commence with raps, feeble at first, and gradually becoming louder. They are of a very varied character, and are heard not only on the table, but on the walls, floor, etc. It has happened to me to witness the development of communications by means of rope struck in different parts of the room in response to the spelling of the French alphabet. I have also remained under the table with a light in my hand, and have heard them sounding distinctly on the table above my head; while at the same time, my observations convinced me of the immobility of Hume, whose hands were resting on the table.

"The first time when I observed the phenomenon of an alteration of weight was in February. This phenomenon was investigated with much care, and the evidence of the reality was convincing. We were ten in number, seated around a large and heavy table, in a well-lighted apartment. Each of us successively verified the fact that the table would become light or heavy at request. At the following séance, also held with Aksakov, I presented myself with a dynamometer. The weight of the table before the séance was 100 lbs. On my request, in the course of the séance, that the table should be made lighter, the dynamometer first marked 50 lbs., and afterwards the tension on it diminished to 35 lbs., and finally to 30 lbs. Immediately afterwards, in response to the expression of my wish that the table should become heavy, the tensions increased to 145 lbs. The alteration in the resistance of the weight fluctuated between the limits of a minimum of 30 lbs. and a maximum of 150 lbs. It was impossible for Hume to render the table heavier by any pressure on it, as he only touched it with the tips of his fingers. But, even admitting that it had been in his power, how would such pressure explain the fact of the table immediately afterwards becoming much lighter than its normal weight? The evident inaction of Hume, who sat in full light, was visible to all the persons present.

"The first occasion on which I saw movement without contact was at a séance of Hume in a brilliantly lit room; the silk dress of a lady seated between Mr. Hume and myself was forcibly shaken. In order to observe better, I knelt down and verified that past doubt the movement which was occurring close under my eyes, observing at the same time the attitude of Hume. I also saw at another of his séances, which was held in my own house, the movement without contact of an object much heavier than a silk skirt. This was the armchair of my study, which I saw move untouched up to the table at which we were seated, and after having approached it, made a detour in order to fix itself in a vacant space between Mr. Hume and another person. A moment afterwards, Hume took a small bell, which was on the table, and held it near the edge of the table and in full view. He presently relinquished his hold, and the bell remained suspended in the air, isolated from all contact. The persons seated near could watch it moving in space; and as for myself, who sat opposite Hume, by rising from my seat I was also enabled to follow its movements. It finished by descending and placing itself on Hume's knees; but presently, without having been touched, it rose anew in the air and settled on the armchair, which had moved forward untouched, and was now standing before our table. Another evening, when I found myself in Hume's company at the house of a relative, and without there being any question of a séance, we were surprised, in the middle of our conversation, to hear raps being struck on the table, and also on an object which being of metal, gave forth the sounds very distinctly. This unsuspected manifestation caused us to start a séance in full light, like all the others had been. Hardly were we seated when manifestation commenced with great power and in great variety; finally a small table which was standing at the other end of the apartment in a corner opposite Hume, left the place by itself and advanced towards us where we were sitting.

"As for touches, I have felt them repeatedly and very distinctly during séances with Hume, and I have often had objects taken from my hands and transported to other persons present at the séance. A ring was drawn from my finger and again replaced on it, and a pencil and a handkerchief were taken from me while Hume's hands were resting on the table before our eyes. I particularly experienced this kind of manifestation during a séance held at my own home in January1872, in the presence of several persons. Fingers like those of a small baby's hand, and warm as in life, touched my hand and sought to draw from it a small bell which I was holding under the table. On letting go my hold, it did not fall, but moved about under the table, ringing all the while. Facts witnessed under such conditions completely convinced me."[17]

Professor Butlerov's article caused a sensation which was heightened in intensity when Professor N.N. Wagner published his own account of séances with Mr. Hume in the prestigious "Revue de L'Europe." Some excerpts from his revelations follow:

"It was with the greatest incredulity and distrust of the phenomena of spiritualism that I accepted the invitation of the Professor of Chemistry, A. von Butlerov, to take part in a séance with Mr. Hume, who was then staying with him in St. Petersburg. One evening, accordingly, I presented myself, but Mr. Hume was unwell. I proposed that we should try a séance without his presence; I selected a table which had never been utilized for this kind of experiment, and we took our places around it to the number of five. Our party consisted of two good friends of mine who had never been present at a séance, Butlerov, a lady, who was excessively fearful that these manifestations might have a diabolic origin, and me.

"We sat with our hands on the table for twenty minutes without anything happening. Suddenly the door opened and Mr. Hume appeared, enveloped in a comforter. 'Ah,' he said, 'so this is what is going on.'

"'No,' I answered. 'We don't want you here now.'

"'Allow me to stay for a few moments,' he asked and took a place beside me.

"Before five minutes had passed the table began to move on my side. Mr. Home, turning his hands palm outwards, placed the backs of them on the table and requested us all to do the same. We complied; but this did not hinder the table from continuing to move. 'Your feet! Where are they?' I asked. After he showed them to me, the table continued to move towards me, pressing me more and more closely.

"This was my first acquaintance with the manifestations. What was passing under my eyes seemed to me rather remarkable. The table was moving without being pushed by anyone; that was plain. No one had any interest in mystifying me; Hume alone might be suspected, but his feet were placed on mine, and his hands, with palms turned outwards, were before my eyes, and I was watching them. I nevertheless formed theories to explain the facts; and where there is no foundations, theories have no longer any substantiation. I came to me that the whole thing was a trick which I could not detect; and I avow that this impression possessed me more strongly than any other; but, on the other hand, it was extremely difficult to conceive of jugglery being practiced under such conditions as were those of the manifestations which occurred with Hume."[18]

Professor Wagner also witnessed the suspension of a bell in the air without support and he heard the rapping of spirits on tables and walls. He concluded his article with the following:

"There remained with me, from all I witnessed, a single incontestable conviction, that the phenomena had taken place. These phenomena sometimes occur in the presence of Hume without the conditions of table and séance; but for their occurrence or non-occurrence he is in no way answerable, for it is not in his power to call them forth. I have been told by

> Mr. Hume himself that manifestations sometimes cease for months at a time.
>
> "I cannot find an explanation for these manifestations either in the unconscious muscular actions by which Faraday tried to account for them twenty years ago, or in the strange theory of 'unconscious cerebration' set forth by Carpenter."

Professor Wagner later published other articles about séances in 1875, which offended non-believers of spiritualism and enthralled those who believed. The reaction to the articles was so great that the Physical Society of the University of St. Petersburg formed a commission of twelve noted scientists under the leadership of the famous chemist D.I. Mendeleev to investigate spiritualistic matters. The scientist Mendeleev explained the motives of the commission as follows:[19]

> "The time has come to turn our attention to the widespread spiritualistic phenomena making place in family circles and among scholars. The business of table rapping, conversations with unseen creatures with the help of knocks, the calling up of human spirits through mediums threatens a spreading of mysticism which is capable of hindering healthy thought and strengthening superstition among the public."[20]

The scientific commission engaged A.N. Aksakov who had published a translation of some articles by Sir William Crookes in 1874 and whose life will be more thoroughly reported in the next chapter. Aksakov visited England in the hope of finding excellent mediums that might be able to convince the commission. His efforts were described by a Mr. Hudson Tuttle in the *Religious Philosophical Journal* in America. Mr. Tuttle wrote: "Hearing favorable reports of the medium ship of the Petty family at Newcastle-on-Tyne, the manifestations occurring behind a pendant curtain, in front of which the mediums were seated, he (Aksakov) visited the family; and his experiences were so satisfactory that he engaged the father and two sons. Unfortunately, by the change of conditions and the absence of the mother, who was the principal medium, the mediumistic forces were not sufficiently powerful to produce any results. After four séances, Aksakov, seeing the hopelessness of the attempts, discontinued the séances and dismissed the mediums. He then engaged an English lady with remarkable mediumistic faculties and offered her services to the commission. This lady, not being a professional medium, desired to remain unknown, and she was presented to the committee under the name of Mrs. Mayer . . . the production of the physical manifestations in the plain light wholly answered Aksakov's expectations, and he at last thought that the necessary medium for presentation to the committee had been found. She, at first, declined the offer, but yielded to his urgent solicitation, and arrived in St. Petersburg in mid-winter, accompanied by her two daughters, whom she would not trust to the hands of strangers.

"The second series of official séances commenced before the committee in January 1876. The manifestations began at the first séance. The rapping was plain and distinct, and of the same character as those which first arrested the attention of the world . . . the tipping and levitation of a table were also produced before the committee. Professor Butlerov and Aksakov attended these séances for the purpose of witnessing the procedures. But alas! In this case, from the beginning, instead of impartial scientific investigation, the committee was determined to prove that phenomena of medium ship had no substantiation. The medium in the words of the judges—who passed judgment before they met at the first séance—made all the manifestations, and Professor Mendeleev, one of the principle personages of the committee, declared that the medium had an instrument concealed in her skirts, to which she resorted. Thus terminated the scientific investigation of spiritualism in Russia."[21]

When the commission declared spiritualism to be a hoax, a large outcry of disapproval took place. One hundred and thirty prominent personages signed a protest which was printed in the *Journal de St. Petersburg* on May 18, 1877. [22] The protestors maintained that the committee had not carried out the requirements it had agreed to at the beginning of the investigation. The commission had agreed to hold at least forty séances, but had held only eight. The execution of the séances was called "superficial" and not properly representative. New examinations were requested as an "important public service."[23] The commission, however, never renewed its investigations.

Mr. Hume's visit and the séances of other foreign mediums aroused the attention of several famous Russian authors. A. K. Tolstoy developed a friendship with Hume and corresponded with him. That the writer believed in spiritualistic forces is evident from the following letter to the critic B.M. Markevich: "Paris . . . I received a letter from D.D. Hume from London which invites me to visit him. His child possesses the same power as he himself and those that are near to him have already seen its manifestations. Where were you when Hume came to my estate? I don't know what sort of opinions you have in regards to spirits; but even if you doubt, you would have believed that time, even more so since the phenomena took place even after his departure. I have spoken about them too much to begin all over again . . . but you should know that the dress of Sophia noticeably swelled, that her sleeves quivered exactly as if from the wind; that I myself felt as if a child's hand had touched my knee and began to drum, and others heard the sound; that tables rose up and hovered above the floor in the air; that two heavy armchairs moved by themselves from one end of the room to the table; that in the evening, several people already lying in bed, saw their blanket rise up and fill with air during the complete absence of a draft."[24]

Tolstoy did not try to explain the phenomena that occurred at his country estate, but merely expressed his belief that they were real. Many other members of the higher circles of the aristocracy were also quite taken with séances. Miss A.F. Tiutchev described another meeting in which the spirits allowed her to stay in the room: "Yesterday I attended one of the most curious things in the world: namely a séance with Mr. Hume . . . I was witness to all the curious phenomena that I had heard about. The table, on which we had lightly placed our hands, raised above the floor to a significant height, bowed to the right and left, while neither the lamp or pencil or other objects on it moved from their place. Even the flame of the lamp did not wave. The table answered with strikes: one signified 'no' two times, sometimes three times, 'yes,' but five times signified that it demanded an alphabet, and then it indicated the letters by knocks. I received answers to all of my questions by means of strikes under my chair, and since my chair was made of straw, I slightly felt the strikes as well as heard them. I first asked the table if it was a spirit. It answered that it was the spirit of a dead person and demanded an alphabet; but it later indicated that it would write only for Prince Savored and for him wrote that name Frederick. Asking the questions I started with the familiar 'thou' and it became mad, knocking very strongly, demanded the alphabet and dictated to me, 'You may speak familiarly only with God!' Someone then came in and disturbed us and the revelations of the spirits ceased. Later they resumed. We saw how an accordion held by Mr. Hume began to play by an unseen hand. The music was touching church refrains. It played also in the hands of Mrs. Mastodon and Princess Dolgoruky. We heard the rustling of a hand through the silk dress of the Princess Dolgoruky and by that means answers of 'yes' and 'no' were given freely. I felt as if someone had seized me strongly on the knees. All the time all in attendance sensed icy air on their hands and feet . . . One of my first questions to the spirit was whether it could manifest in a chair as well as in the table. It said 'yes.' When Count Adleberg left the room, the table began to spin, and when they asked it why, asked that Count Adleberg return since he helped the manifestations. All the strikes on the table took place with incredible speed; they were not the movements that a person would make. Even several people couldn't have lifted such a heavy table. It was either magnetic phenomenon unknown as yet or it was a supernatural phenomenon. But in any case, one asked oneself, why were the phenomena so stupid? If the devil was involved, he would have had to be smarter. The table only spoke general phrases and made flat remarks. It never mentioned the past or the world of the spirits, or about the future, or about something secret like what evil spirits try to do in order to deceive the curious mind. It only communicated: "I am called so and so," and "I know you." Or "I don't know you." Generally, it was a most stupid conversation. Never did I hear anything worthy of attention in the revelations or the spirits . . . The most curious thing in my opinion was the great clock with the playing monkeys on it. After the last séance of Mr. Hume in Tsarskoe, it awoke me in the middle of the night by its action. Yet it had not been wound up. That same clock was brought here and placed on a buffet table. It was not wound up nor had it played since then. Today its movement started again even though no one touched it. By the way, the machine is wound with great difficulty with a thick key: only then will the monkeys play on their instruments. This incident, I must say, aroused in me an unpleasant feeling. During the séance, on the other hand, I was not afraid; I was more inclined to humor and laughter: only once when I felt a touch, I involuntarily screamed. I asked myself, 'Is there something in this bad or not?' As a time-passing activity it seems harmless, but anyway, I was afraid that there was some sort of hidden deceit. Nevertheless, it was all so amusing and curious. How can one solve these questions?"[25]

Miss Tiutchev was not the only one skeptical of the events that took place at Mr. Hume's séances. Famous writers as I.S. Turgenev and L.N. Tolstoy also saw the medium work and expressed doubt about his verisimilitude. Mr. Hume was, however, responsible for a minor literary motif in Russian literature: the medium.

I.S. Turgenev

When Mr. Hume's popularity was at its height in the 1890s, I.S. Turgenev began to revise an old work entitled "Specters," a fantastic story in which the author flies over Moscow and other places with the spirit of a beautiful lady named Alice. The tale had been written in 1856 for publication in *The Russian Herald*, but a dispute with the editor M. Katkov had caused the writer to set the work aside.[26] In 1863 an acquaintance, N.V. Shcherban, gave Turgenev some suggestions to improve the story,[27] but the novelist wrote to A.A. Fet that the tale still "has no human sense."[28] Finally Turgenev sent the literary piece to P.V. Annenkov with the following note: "Read this rubbish and see if . . . it's wise to publish this joke."[29] The editor F.M. Dostoevsky realizing the public's interest in spiritualism, decided to publish and the author agreed. Later Dostoevsky mercilessly parodied "Specters" in his novel *The Devils*.

Before "Specters" was published, Turgenev added the following explanation for his readers:

> "All real works of art must stand by themselves, on their own legs—and therefore do not need preliminary explanations and interpretations. Not being sure that "Specters" belongs to works of that sort. I ask the reader who, perhaps, is right to expect something more serious from me, not to look at this fantasy as any sort of allegory or to try and find hidden meanings, but simply to see in it a series of pictures bound together rather superficially."

In spite of the introductory remarks, the critics heaped abuse on the famous writer. The humorist D. Minaev wrote a dramatic spoof in which Mephistopheles asks Faust if he has read "Specters." He answers, "Maybe, I've read a lot of trash."[30]

Another critic in the journal *Spark* wrote a conversation between "Daydream" and "Nonsense" which revealed that Turgenev was not flying over Moscow with Alice, but in bed with "Daydream" herself.[31] The phantom Alice also has been called Turgenev's muse.[32] While the story brought the famous author rebuke, it was not his only story on such a theme. Other demonic stories followed: "Knock, Knock, Knock" and "Clara Milich."

Turgenev had a long friendship with the French writer of supernatural tales Prosper Mérimée, but the Russian author himself was never greatly interested in the occult. He is known to have said, "To everything supernatural—I am indifferent." However, he did use spiritualism to belittle literary figures in his novel, *Smoke*. The hero of the book, Litvinov, loved two women at the same time. The first, his fiancé, was a typical Turgenev heroine: lovely, charming and fine, with no esoteric interests. The other heroine Irina who was a member of a high court circle liked the unusual. When the author wanted to display the superficiality of the society figure and the members of her court circle, he showed their interest in spiritualism by having a medium perform at one of their evening parties (chapter fifteen). The Countess Lise, after telling about her strange experiences with the famous D.D. Hume, who caused tables to move and instruments to play by themselves, asked a medium named Fox to show them some evidence of magnetism. The fictitious Mr. Fox, however, was not as successful as the real Mr. Hume had been. When a live lobster was placed before the medium, he was not able to stop its movements by magnetism. The countess comforted the spiritualist by saying that "Even Mr. Hume had unsuccessful presentations." Later the "Queen of the Wasps" told about a séance with Mr. Hume in which hands crawled over her. She claimed that she could even see the hands and put her ring on one of their fingers. The conversation of the entire evening was trivial and belittling. Turgenev used spiritualism only to present negative aspects in a literary heroine.

Turgenev again rebuked mediums in "A Strange Story" (1870), but the tale about a gracious girl who left home to follow a medium on his travels also criticized life in Russia and brought the writer considerable censure in the press.[36] The novelist's disrespect for spiritualism is also seen in a letter to V.P. Polonskii from Paris in which a reference is made to a Monsieur Bredive, a medium who was having sensational success in St. Petersburg. Turgenev wrote: "Bredive—to our present deaf and empty time—would naturally cause a lot of turbulence in Petersburg—it's the order of things. Even here mediums and somnambulists are supported by Russians."[37]

In St. Petersburg, N.P. Wagner described a séance of the popular spiritualist Monsieur Bredive in *The Herald of Europe* in 1872:[38] "In October I was invited by Mr. Aksakov and Mr. Butlerov to attend the séance of another medium, Mr. Camille Bredive . . . who belonged to the number of professional mediums; that is, those who hired themselves out for séances. He was a Frenchman from Paris who sold porcelain and who tried to enrich his own pockets by making use of the mediumistic abilities nature had given him. He was a young man, not tall, with a somewhat well-formed, kind, but trivial face and lively black eyes. Understandably, his appearance was of such a type that he inspired little trust. And it was necessary to control his hands and feet so as to be sure that the phenomena that occurred were not accomplished by them. I shall speak here only of the phenomena that took place when the medium's hands and feet were under the control of the guests.

"The table raised one and three-fourths inches, then fifteen and even to half a yard from the floor, and then momentarily fell again. But sometimes it remained in that position several moments and some time remained in the air for twenty seconds. Two times I witnessed how the table completely flew into the air. Both times the room was dark or else light came through an open door from an adjoining room. During the rising of the table, all the participators had to rise from their palaces. The first time Bredive hastily placed both his hands on my head, shouting, "Here are my hands" with the aim of convincing me that he had nothing to do with the table's movement. The second time, I quickly felt with my foot, but the table was such that he could not have raised it with his foot.

"The movement of things was the most remarkable proof of the authenticity of Bredive's powers. A rather large table which stood behind me and was more than twenty-eight inches from the table of the séance, suddenly quickly moved toward us and hit me in the back hard enough to leave a mark on the spine of my chair . . . Allow me to stop here and say that . . . . I am deeply convinced of the veracity of mediumistic phenomena."

Articles such as the above caused considerable discussion in nineteenth-century literary salons. L.N. Tolstoy was particularly distressed by the credence given to spiritualism in such writings.

L.N. Tolstoy

The creator of *War and Peace* and *Anna Karenina* was too much of a rationalist to be carried away by the Russian interest in spiritualism. In his writings he scorned the occult science, but, like his friend Turgenev, he was interested in mediums in his youth. In 1857 in Paris Tolstoy attended a séance of the famous Mr. Hume, which the writer recorded in his diary in two short sentences: "Hume neither did nor did not do anything. I ought to try it myself."[39] There is no record that the author did try any spiritualistic experiments, but there is much in his writings which shows his criticism of séances and mediums.

When the noted zoologist N.P. Wagner's article "On the Subject of Spiritualism" was published, Tolstoy was appalled.[40] The scientist gave many incredible descriptions of séances, especially the type called "face séance" in which the medium was placed behind a curtain while a table pounded out messages from spirits.[41] Tolstoy did not believe the veracity of the experiments and was disturbed that such an outstanding scientist could believe in the occult science.[42]

Tolstoy's disdain for mediums was expressed in a comment he wrote on the back of the fourth page of an article called "Spiritualism and Mediums," which appeared in *The Russian News*. Tolstoy scribbled: "Observations, experience, facts, inductive method. Inductive, deductive are only words relative to the essence of thought. This difference or opposition has sense only in regard to details (ways) of a dialectic of thought, but not relative to the essence of the thought. That is, I can prove or show something inductively or deductively, but the thought comes to me or appears to me neither inductively or deductively. So it is impossible for a thought to take place inductively. In order to make experiments, one must already have an 'aim' for the experiments; in order to see the facts one must see what they prove. Such phenomena as mediums only prove the poverty of the mind of the people who support them. Thought is the aim of spiritualistic experiences. But such thought is superstition, that is, the absence of wisdom."[43]

Later the writer received a letter from N.N. Starched, a critic, who mentioned that he was preparing to write about spiritualism. He added, "I propose that spiritualism is based on our striving toward the irrational and that it is being sought incorrectly."[44] Tolstoy answered, "I was amazed . . . that you are writing about spiritualism. I almost didn't write about it. My article is ready."[45] The article Tolstoy referred to has never been found.

Tolstoy did allow a ghostly spirit to enter his literature in the short story "Polikushka." An evil spirit manifested itself in the form of the suicide victim Pokikey in order to frighten Dutlow, the possessor of the dead man's money. Tolstoy used the spirit for its dramatic effect, having heard the tale from an acquaintance in Brussels.[46] In another story, "Kholstomer," the spirit of a dead horse talks about his past, but the account does not seem in the realm of the supernatural. However, there is a tale supposedly told by Tolstoy which was not included in the ninety-one volume collection of Tolstoy's works. In 1910 there *Rebus*, a spiritualistic journal which will be discussed later, reported (n. 5, 5) a story by Tolstoy which had been printed in the newspaper *The Russian Morning*. The tale was supposedly told by the great Russian writer as an example of the supernatural and was written down by a guest. The following translation is probably the first in English: "It occurred some years ago on Christmas Eve. E. A. B—s was planning to visit me (Tolstoy) from a neighboring estate. We were expecting her toward evening on the twenty-fourth, but she arrived, distraught and upset, on Christmas morning. Upon arrival she explained that she had almost perished on the way, having lost the road and ending up in a forest. The details were as follows: in the morning when she set out, the weather was beautiful and sunny, but after an hour and a half, the wind picked up, snow began falling and everything was suddenly enswathed in a blizzard.

They were blinded by the whiteness and the road was soon covered. Soon it was evident that they had lost the way and were circling about.

"The coachman was a timid and indecisive type, but the young lady was hot tempered and impatient and goaded the driver. Finally the coachman became mad from her orders and, having stopped the horses, exclaimed, 'I'll not go farther!' and slipped down from the driver's seat.

The young lady began shouting and abusing him, but he stood on his own, refused to go farther and began unharnessing the horses.

"'What are you doing?' she asked, condescendingly.

"'Makes no difference whether they die moving or standing! And it's easier for cattle to die standing.' And from where he had found such decisiveness and courage, God knows! The young lady objected, but he unharnessed the horses, moved them together, raised their shafts, crossed himself earnestly and sat down alongside them on the snow. The impatient agitation of the young lady turned to fear.

"'Is death really possible?' flashed through her mind and her body trembled from a cold shiver. 'You should look for the road,' she timidly said to the coachman. 'You might find it.'

"'Search? Well, why not?' answered the coachman. 'Except that it's no good. If the time to die's come, then we'll die, and it won't do any good to find the road.' However, the coachman stood and was quickly lost in the snowy winds.

"The young lady remained alone; fear seized her whole being, darkness was setting in unmercifully all around, and snowy hills seemed to approach and look at her coldly and dispassionately. 'White, cold death,' she thought, and closed her eyes. In the dark she saw bright, bouncing fiery circles and floating reddish lakes. 'The end, the end,' she whispered. 'My God, and on such an evening, Christmas Eve, and suddenly, the end.' And as happens on the eve of one's life, all the details of her disorderly and colorful past seemed to flash by like a long movie film, and all her life there had been nothing beautiful, great, significant or important; there had only been from the beginning to the end an expectation of something fine and extraordinary. 'And now there will be nothing, and nothing to expect, everything is over.'

"'Can't find the road!' resounded to her ears and the figure of the coachman advanced from the snowy fog.

"'It means we're lost?' whispered the young lady, half inquisitively, half assuredly.

"'We've lived enough, evidently,' the coachman abruptly pronounced and again sat down on the snow by the horses.

"It grew dark. The snowy hills came up to the carriage and bowed low.

"'Oh Lord God,' suddenly came loudly and passionately from the young lady. 'I believe in you and know that You see me. I do believe, I do believe.' And she heartfully cried.

"'My lady, Elena Aleksandrovna, look! A fire!' the coachman shouted and jumped up.

"In the snowy mist a reddish flaming dot was shining.

"'Let's go!' In a few minutes the horses were harnessed and the carriage, once it was freed from the snow that had stuck to its sides, was soon moving toward the flaming spot. They drove a long time, but the reddish dot did not disappear. Finally it brightly flashed and a lantern appeared in the gloom. They had arrived at the gate of a small peasant's hut. A lad was standing, holding a bright lantern on a long pole.

"'At last,' he said, opening the gate. 'I was tired of waiting.'

"'But how did you know?' the young lady asked in surprise.

"'But why wouldn't I?' The old man came from you and ordered a lantern lit up,' answered the lad as he led the horses into the court.

"'An old man?' she replied in amazement, but her tiredness and weariness from what she had lived through did not allow her to pursue the matter for the moment.

"Awakening the next morning, significantly calmed, the young lady recalled all the details of the preceding night. 'Old man? What old man?' she asked herself realizing the extent of what had happened. 'And how could a lantern shine so far in a snowstorm?' She went to the young man and asked, 'What old man came to you? I sent no one!'

"'I don't know. Just some little old kind man with a white beard down to his belt came up and said, "The young lady's coach has left the road. Light a lantern."'

"'An old man?' the young lady repeated, lost in thought.

"'He was a sort of strange guy,' continued the boy. 'He didn't stop and warm himself or ask for shelter. He just came up to the window, knocked and left after he said it.'

"The young lady came to me and related the event. We expressed 'ohs' and 'ahs' as she told the story, but more from her excitement and concern than from the news about the old man.

"That evening the young lady could not sleep. She could only think about what had happened: the old man and the lantern. While thinking she suddenly glanced at the icon of Nicholas the Miracle Worker: a soft aura was shining around it. The lips of the holy image began speaking softly and the young lady heard most clearly, 'It was I who order the lantern.'"

Tolstoy became silent. A quietness settled on the room, broken only by someone's breathing. "There's the miraculous for you," Tolstoy said and turned to Sofia Andreevna, "Could I have some tea with a butter cookie? I'll go to my room and work a bit."

Usually Tolstoy used spiritualism in his literature to show his disapproval of mediums and the supernatural. The nineteenth-century's compassion for spirits and mediums was best explained by the author in *Anna Karenina*. In chapter fourteen, part one, of the novel, when Levin denies that there is a spiritualistic force, Vronsky interrupts and gives the most well-known argument:

"So you won't admit that there is something to it. But why not? We admit the existence of electricity which we certainly don't know anything about. Why can't there be then some new force as yet unknown to us? The spiritualists now say that we don't know what this force is, but there is such a force and it does operate under certain conditions. Let the scientists find out what this force is. No, I don't see why there shouldn't be a new force."

Tolstoy ridiculed Vronsky by having him speak favorably of the esoteric science. Later when the author also wanted to belittle Karenin, he had the jilted husband fall under the influence of a clairvoyant named Landau who had been so highly accepted by Petersburg society that one woman had adopted him as her son. Karenin did not make a move without consulting the mystic (part seven, chapters 20-21). To accentuate the absurdity of Karenin's pre-occupation with the medium, Tolstoy arranged for the sophisticated Stiva Oblonsky to visit one of the séances held by Landau. Sensing the skepticism of the visitor, the medium requested that Oblonsky leave. Tolstoy indicated that Karenin was so taken in by the charlatan that he did not realize that Landau was protecting his own interests by having Oblonsky depart.

Tolstoy also belittled the upper class through the supernatural in two other novels. In *War and Peace* he degraded the aristocracy when Ippolit Kuragin asked if the group he joined at an evening party was telling ghost stories (book one, part one, chapter three). The implication was that such a petty activity was common among the assembled aristocrats. In the novel *Resurrection*, Tolstoy showed his hatred of a general who was the director of a St. Petersburg prison by having him pass his time in supernatural games. When the hero of the book, Prince Nekliudov, went to see him on important matters, the general was engaged in answering the question, "How do the souls of the departed recognize one another after death?" He sought the answer by placing his hands on a saucer in front of an alphabet: expecting a higher power to spell out the words (chapter nineteen).

In the play "The Fruits of Enlightenment," Tolstoy continued to discredit aristocratic society by having a peasant girl trick her masters in a séance. A major figure of the play, Leonid Fedorovich Zvezdintsev, a sixty-year-old retired lieutenant of the horse guards, earnestly believed in mediums and had a séance for his guests. Tania, a peasant servant, performed and the host and the guests were very pleased with the success of the meeting. When the peasant girl confessed to her conspiracy, one of the guests, a professor, refused to believe that the girl was the cause of the spiritual manifestations. He even said, "It is very probable that what this girl did simply evoked the materialization of the mediumistic energy—giving it definite form." Tolstoy wanted to show that people who believed in spiritualism accepted it blindly, even when it was proven false. The same opinion was held by another great Russian writer: Dostoevsky.

F.M. Dostoevsky

An interest in the esoteric is evident in Dostoevsky's life and works. The great writer attended séances, wrote criticism about the short stories of Edgar Allan Poe, and used fanciful dreams in realistic fiction to enliven his characterizations, a technique he inherited from Pushkin. Spiritualism attracted Dostoevsky as a young man. He attended a séance when the medium L.N. Livchak did a rope trick which caused several noted scientists considerable embarrassment.[47] The botanist V.I. Butlerov wrote that the event was the "result of an enormous technical operation that required significant mental power." Later the medium admitted that his great "technical operation" was done simply by "breaking a circled rope. Then, after tying the knots together, the broken parts were mended."[48] Evidently he substituted the knotted rope for the unknotted when nobody observed. Dostoevsky himself said that there was some logical explanation besides the popular "fourth dimension theory."[49]

In his personal life, Dostoevsky gave evidence of his curiosity about psychic phenomena. Doctor Janovsky, who treated the author, reported that Dostoevsky believed in premonitions and related the following incident. During the second year of their acquaintance, the doctor lived in Pavlovsk, returning to St. Petersburg three times a week for his medical practice. One day a strange urge convinced him of the necessity of returning to the city for an unscheduled visit. In a remote area he accidentally ran into Dostoevsky, who had no money to pay a petty debt demanded of him by some military clerk. When the writer saw the doctor, he shouted, "See! See who will save me!" Later Dostoevsky called the incident remarkable and every time he would remember it, he would say, "Well, after that, how could one not believe in premonitions?"[50]

Dostoevsky often discussed spiritualism with friends,[51] and in 1876, he published his thoughts about spirits in "The Diary of a Writer":[52] "I think that a person who wants to believe in spiritualism cannot be hindered by anything, neither by lectures nor by entire commissions: and the disbeliever, if he really does not wish to believe, cannot be persuaded by anything. That is exactly the sort of persuasion I overcame at the February séance at A.N. Aksakov's, at least during the first strong impression. Since then, I have simply denied spiritualism, that is, in essence I have been indignant over the mystical aspect of its doctrine. (After reading the report of the academic commission's study of spiritualism, I could never be in a position to deny the spiritual phenomena which I have been acquainted with even before the séance with the medium and now, especially now.) But after that remarkable séance I suddenly guessed, or more so, suddenly realized that it's not enough that I don't believe in spiritualism, but besides that, I don't want to believe—so no sort of proof will ever shake my position."

There is, however, an account, unpublished before in English, by an acquaintance of Dostoevsky, who maintained that the Russian writer did give credence to spiritualistic phenomena. In 1885 the *Rebus* (n. 26, 240-241) printed the memoirs of a Ms. V. P.— va, who gave some interesting insights into Dostoevsky's attitude toward the occult science. The authenticity of these accounts could be suspect, but the following is a translation of Ms. P—va's report: "I remember once during the sixth week of Lent, when I was intending to return to Moscow from St. Petersburg, I dropped in on the Dostoevskys for a farewell greeting. Fedor Mikhailovich's wife was not at home and he himself met me in their entranceway, explaining that he could not receive me at the moment even though he would like to discuss spiritualism with me, because he was in such a hurry to expedite his diary. 'But it's a shame you're leaving,' he added, 'when you've no reason to be going now. Wait for Holy Week here, as I'm intending to do, and come to us on Easter; we'll have a talk.'

"It turned out that I did remain and at the end of Holy Week, I went to the Dostoevskys at his invitation. Again Fedor Mikhailovich himself met me, and as I comprehended from his first glance, he was not pleased with my arrival. His face was more sullen then I had ever seen it. 'I don't want to talk about spiritualism' were his first words. 'You've come in vain.'

"Not a little taken aback by such a greeting, I smiled and said that I had not come to see him, but to visit Anna Grigorievna, who appeared at that moment in the entranceway, and, somewhat confused by the conduct of her husband, invited me to enter. Having seated me, she immediately began speaking about spiritualism. Fedor Mikhailovich disappeared, but five minutes had not passed before he returned with his usual glass of tea in his hands and sat down at the table near us, listening to our conversation.

"When I related some events from a rather successful séance in our circle, he said, 'That's all nonsense, just your fantasy.' Or something like that, and he began an account of a séance that he had experienced. In a circle of close friends there was once a table-raising experience during which the table actually moved, rocked, knocked out by its leg suitable answers even to rather apprehensive questions, and then went through the whole long room first rising up from the floor and continuing to move through the air, and then again settling down on the floor.

"'Whatever caused that, Fedor Mikhailovich?' I asked. 'Was it some sort of artificial contraption or deceit? Your acquaintances evidently had it all set up.'

"'You are forgetting,' he answered almost angrily. 'I just said that this occurred among very close friends who would not think of trying to deceive me.'

"'But then how can you explain such phenomena, which you yourself deny, if you don't allow deceit in the matter?'

"Not answering a single word, Dostoevsky, completely vexed, practically ran out of the room and returned to the living room only after we had begun talking about something else. However, during my departure, he supported the request of his wife to have the opportunity of being present at one of the séances of our circle."

It would be interesting to hear Fedor Mikhailovich give an in depth analysis of his own contradictory feelings in regard to spiritualism. Of course, as he himself said on that matter, he did not like mystical explanations of facts, but then why was he uncontrollably drawn sometimes into conversations about questions which were evidently antipathetic to his views, and at other times, wouldn't even listen to them? Why such a double standard? Perhaps he himself couldn't have given a reasonable answer to such a question. I would say that the reason for his attitude was an involuntary and an undesired recognition of not only the reality of opposing fact to his personal insights, but mainly an involuntary recognition of an important meaning for mankind in its contemporary condition, where it is ruled by materialism. Fedor Mikhailovich did not want such a meaning and explanation, but his own artificial denial didn't always work for him when, apart from his will, he himself felt that his explanation was artificial. Spiritualism aggravated him, but also attracted him. But never, at least from what I heard from him, did he ever show a serious attitude toward it. Yet this is what he said about it in his "Diary" in the April issue of 1876: "Reading the account (from the commission under the direction of the chemist Mendeleev), it is beginning to appear to be decisive that our scholars have contemplated spiritualism as it exists in St. Petersburg only in the apartment of A. N. Aksakov and they seem to know nothing about the thirst for it which has appeared in our society or about the reasons why it has begun spreading among us Russians; but they all knew this and have simply avoided it. But, having been organized into a commission, these scholars have become public figures and are no longer just private persons. They have received a commission and therefore, it appears, did not wish to take it into consideration, but simply sat down at the spiritualistic table, continuing completely as before to be private persons, that is, they sit laughing, mocking, giggling, and are even a bit perturbed that they must take seriously something so silly. It might be, however, that the entire house, or the entire apartment of A.N. Aksakov is equipped with springs and ropes, and that the medium has some kind of a machine which clicks between his knees (about this clever invention the commission was informed later by N.F. Wagner). Yet, you see, every serious spirit (Oh, do not laugh at these words, for it is a serious matter) will ask, having read the account of the commission: 'How is it possible that in that house where I know everyone so well—my children, wife, relatives and acquaintances—that the very same phenomena should always take place: a table rocks, rises, noises are heard, and intelligent answers are given.' For you see, I know for sure that in my house there are no machines or ropes, and that my wife and children would not think of deceiving me. But the high-level commission doesn't allow such a thought, nor does it even suggest the following: 'Those who believe in it are simply flippant or poorly educated people.'"

"Let's say that I am flippant and poorly educated," Answers Dostoevsky later in the name of that serious spirit, "but I have no machine that clicks: I know for sure there's not one in my home, and I don't even have the means by which I could order such amusing instruments: and whoever is selling them is unknown to me, and how does the clicking take place in our home anyway? You say that we ourselves somehow press on the table unconsciously; but I assure you that we aren't such children and watch ourselves carefully and we especially watch that we don't press on the table; we do our experiments with curiosity and impartiality. . . . No, such a sudden and hurried decision by the commission on such an important point of research and concluded from such destructive experiments is too supercilious and hardly scientific."

It is not true that in these words, put into the mouth of a serious spirit, there is evidence of the author's conviction of the reality of phenomena which were suggested to me involuntarily in a private conversation? Certainly, Dostoevsky without doubt believed in spiritualistic facts, believed even in their mystical interpretations, and therefore reacted to them hostilely, preferring to give such interpretations his own shading, in agreement with his spiritual world-view in general.

Village of Vladykino, 10 June 1885

Books in Dostoevsky's private library give further evidence of the author's interest in the occult science:[53] for instance, *Experimental Researches on Spiritualism*, by Professor R. Gera (1866); and *Spiritualism and Science: Experimental Researches on the Psychic Force*, by William Crookes (1872).

Dostoevsky also showed his curiosity in the esoteric by his publication of stories by Edgar Allan Poe in the journal *Vremia* (time) and in articles about the American writer's literary style. Dostoevsky was intrigued by Poe's technique of presenting the outward possibility of an unnatural event while proceeding to relate a realistic tale. In the issue of *Vremia* that contains the stories "The Tell-Tale Heart," "The Black Cat," and "The Devil in the Belfry," there is an unsigned piece entitled "St. Petersburg Dreams in Verse and Prose." The work was by Dostoevsky as it is an autobiographical account of a writer which parallels the Russian author's life. An imprisonment in Siberia is referred to as a "journey to the moon," which could indicate just how much Dostoevsky made Poe's images his own.[54]

Dostoevsky like Poe, often intermingled naturalistic and irrational elements. In "The Double" (1846) Dostoevsky explained the hero's talking with his own image as a case of mental imbalance. In "The Landlady" (1847), the heroine gave the impression of being possessed by the devil, but the author again explained her problems as an example of psychological imbalance. In "Netochka Nevanova" (1848), a clarinetist inherited a remarkable violin and became obsessed by the power the devil had over him when he played. The evil powers of these early stories by

Dostoevsky were based on the folkloric devils of Russian fables and Western short stories, and the author continued using devils in his major prose writings: for instance, Father Ferapont's multiple devils in *The Brothers Karamazov*. However, the influence of spiritualism is also evident in the esoteric aspects of the great novels. In *Crime and Punishment* there is a discussion of ghosts between Svidrigailov and Raskolnikov (part four, chapter one) Which would have been inspired by Dostoevsky's knowledge of séances. When Svidrigailov tells Raskolnikov about his dead wife's visitations, the descriptions are similar to the spiritualistic visits during a séance. Marfa Petrovna appears only briefly and speaks a few trifling remarks. Her oral utterances are similar to the phrases in thousands of séances recorded in the nineteenth century. They are pointless and disappointing to the listener. The same is true of the momentary visitation and pointless comments. Dostoevsky could have remembered his own experiences at séances while writing the scene.

In the novel *The Devils*, Dostoevsky referred to the book *From New York to San Francisco and Back to Russia* by P.I. Ogorodnikov. When Shatov in *The Devils* mentioned his experiences in America, he implied that spiritualism was a part of the American way of life. [55] Ogorodnikov's book was published in 1872 and contained a conversation between two Russians who accidentally met in America and traveled together. Ogorodnikov and a student named A.E. Ia . . . v discussed American spiritualism while on their way to Chicago:[56] "Ia . . . v related that Chicago, except for an abundance of Germans, is remarkable because most of the population is in intercourse with the next world and they are therefore somewhat strange. 'And the practical

American makes peace with that rubbish called the study of spirits?' involuntarily tore from my throat.

"'In America, as in a country with wide freedom of conscience, thought and speech, spiritualism, similarly to a majority of other cults, has found an abundance of followers of spiritualism in the country, and hundreds of remarkable people are in charge of it: lawyers, men of letters and scholars. They have their own special schools, their own religious service, their own festivals, picnics and meetings; they publish many books about spiritualism, their catechism and papers; they have more than clairvoyants, and mediums: their doctors especially medics, can cure by means of spirits any disease of the body or the soul, and for that they charge only two or three dollars; several of them are so gifted they can speak all dead and living languages and create miracles.'

"Having received such an account of the Chicago spiritualists, I reproached my acquaintance for not realizing that I truly doubt everything about the charlatans and exploiters of easily convinced fools.

"'But not all spiritualists belong to the category of rascal,' Ia..v said.

"I proposed to Ia . . . v that we get together at a séance of one of the mediums, but the hour was late, and probably all magicians were busy with beer by that time."

Dostoevsky referred to Ogorodnikov's book because he agreed with the traveler's low opinion of spiritualism. Another reference to the travel book was made in *The Devils* when Shatov discussed labor conditions in America.[57] The writer's mentioning of spiritualism in the novel is unusual because the occult science is rare in his prose writings. He usually expressed the esoteric through dreams.

One of the most famous dreams in Dostoevsky's novels is in *The Brothers Karamazov*: "The Devil: Ivan's Nightmare." There are references to spiritualism in the dream, which take place in candlelight with a demon dressed possibly like a medium. The devil's statements about spiritualism refer to the Western occult science which was so popular in the country. The devil speaks of himself as a spirit and jokes that Ivan seems to think that he is dreaming. At various times Ivan himself calls the demonic visitor a phantom, a hallucination and a ghost. In his *Diary of a Writer* (Jan. 1876, chapter thirty), Dostoevsky associated devils with spiritualism: "I should like to bring my January diary to a close with something more joyful. There is a humorous theme, and it is important; it is in vogue, namely, the topic of devils, of spirits . . . Clergymen are raising their voices; they are instructing science itself not to bother with magic, not to investigate 'that witchery' and if the clergy have raised their voices, it means that the thing has reached momentous proportions . . . But the trouble is: are there devils? . . . My trouble is that I do not believe in devils and it is a pity since I have formed a clear and remarkable theory about spirits, but one basked exclusively on devils; without them my theory is valueless."

Dostoevsky goes into detail in a humorous manner to explain his theory. He states that the basis of the devils' kingdom and that their purpose is to sow discord among us. His definition could well have been taken from Chulkov's eighteenth-century *Dictionary of Russian Superstitions*,[53] which maintains that discord is the *raison d'ê tre* of devils. Dostoevsky concludes that evil spirits had already caused such trouble in the new science of spiritualism; many people had already been persecuted because of their belief in the popular science. The writer referred to the scientific committee on spiritualistic phenomena in St. Petersburg which was discussed earlier. He claimed that devils had already caused such discord in the committee's work; instead of fighting back, the devils had surrendered and had done nothing. Consequently the people who believed that tables could fly had been ridiculed. Then, when the committee turned its back in disgust, the devils had something else that again convinced the adherence of spiritualism that they were correct after all. Of course, such an event caused the proceedings to start all over again. Séances, failure and ridicule, Dostoevsky claimed that it was all working just the way the devils wanted it. He ended his remarks with the following: "Of course I have been jesting and laughing from the first to the last word; however, here is what I wish to say in conclusion: if one is to consider spiritualism as something which has a new creed (and almost all spiritualists, even the sanest among them, are somewhat inclined toward such a view) several of the above remarks could be accepted as true . . . For this reason, may God bring a hasty success to an open investigation by both sides; that alone will eradicate as soon as possible the stench that is going around, and it might enrich science with new discoveries. But the shouting, defaming and expulsion of each other from society because of spiritualism . . . that, in my opinion . . . is intolerance and persecution. And that is precisely what the devils want!"

Devils played a considerable role in Dostoevsky's works. It has been pointed out by Robert Belknap that those evil forces form a veritable subtext in *The Brothers Karamazov*.[59] Dostoevsky's use of devils and spirits is especially evident in the short story "Bobok," which was written toward the end of his career and was included in his *Diary of a Writer* in 1873. "Bobok" is a critic's delight. It has Poe's blending of the irrational with the realistic; the hero overhears the conversation of the dead in a cemetery; it has Hoffman's exaggerations: noises coming from the graves, etc.; it has the decadence of Baudelaire: the dying dead romp in a final orgy of debauchery; and the story has Gogol's mixture of fantasy and morality: the dead question the purpose of their lives and discuss the nature of morality itself. "Bobok" has even been compared stylistically to Gogol's "The Dram of a Madman"[60] There is also reason to believe that Dostoevsky's attendance at séances influenced his writing of the tale. He went to mediumistic meetings during the 1850s and several séances from that period were reported earlier from the memories off Miss Tiutchev the lady-in-waiting at Alexander II's court.[61] Certain aspects of Dostoevsky's story are similar to Miss Tiutchev's descriptions. In both, sounds are muffled. The hero of "Bobok" has trouble discerning the voices from the graves and Miss Tiutchev speaks of the faint sounds of the various phenomena she witnessed. More important is the pointlessness and stupidity of the communication of the spirits. One character in "Bobok" comments that "You can't imagine what an absence of wit there is here;" and a philosopher is noted for muttering a few irrelevant words each week. Other characters use the words "stupid" and "nonsensical" to describe their conversations. Miss Tiutchev concludes that the spirit world is indeed dull because of the absurdity of the spirits. She found the "voices from the other world" to be abusive, foolish and senseless. For her, spiritualism was fascinating, but fatuous. Dostoevsky, it appears, agreed. In fact, "Bobok" could be interpreted as a parody of a séance where the absurd is placed on a par with empirical reality.

While Dostoevsky did not believe in spiritualism, he never ridiculed the occult science in his literary works. His closest rebuke would be the parody mentioned above, "Bobok." Even the famous Kuz'ma Prutkov, the literary pseudonym of the writer A.K. Tolstoy and his cousins, the Zhemchuzhnikov brothers, did not belittle mediums and spirits in his anecdotes and poems. For many authors of the period, spiritualism was on a par with empirical reality.

A.K. Tolstoy

In 1858 A. K. Tolstoy, a distant relative of L.N. Tolstoy, attended séances in the Winter Palace when the spiritualist D.D. Hume acted as medium. The writer developed a friendship with the famous foreigner and visited him in London. A letter during his stay with Hume describes some of the phenomena he witnessed at the medium's residence. Tolstoy wrote:[62] "It is two a.m. and I just returned from Mr. Hume's. In spite of the sorrow of our separation, I do not regret my journey to London since the séances have been stupefying . . . There were many phenomena which you know; after them we continued in the half-darkness; all the furniture moved, turned over even; one table went on top of another; a divan moved completely across the room; a bell walked around the room and rang in the air and so forth. Later there was complete darkness. A piano began to play by itself; a bracelet was taken from the arm of Mrs. Gibson and fell on the table, giving off rays of light. Mr. Hume was raised into the air and I touched his legs when he flew over my head. Hands touched and embraced my knees and took my hands, and when I wanted to take hold of them, they melted. On a table there was a paper and pencils; one sheet of paper slipped into my hand and the alphabet said that I must give it to Mr. Hume. On it was written, 'Aimez-la toujours. N. Kroll.' The handwriting was similar to that of his mother and we compared it with her letters . . . A pillow fell on my head. What amazed me most of all was that hands that squeezed me would melt when I reached for them. A cold wind blew very noticeably around us, but Mr. Hume's hands burned after the séance and his eyes were filled with tears."

An interest in the esoteric is evident in many of Tolstoy's literary creations. His first story, "The Vampire," was based on Gothic horror themes; the damnation of a family line as punishment for some evil deed by an ancestor, hypnotism by a portrait, and vampires. The story brought the young author the critical praise from the critic V. Belinsky, who predicted a fine career for its creator.[63]

Tolstoy wrote other horror stories at the beginning of his career, for instance, "A Meeting after Three Hundred Years" and "Amena," but he did not continue to write on supernatural themes. However, the mysterious and mystical are evident in many of his mature works. In his novel, *Prince Serebrianny*, a clever wizard weaves an element of suspense through the book. He distributes potions, reads visions at a waterfall, and makes gifts of protective amulets. His appearance creates a sense of the mystical which helps develop the atmosphere of the medieval tale. Another major work, the play "Don Juan," begins with a lengthy discussion among spirits about the fate of man. When Satan appears the spirits contest his right to the soul of the hero of the play. By beginning the work with the supernatural beings, the author balanced the esoteric ending of the original tale when the personified statue took the life of Don Juan.

In his serious poems and political ballads, Tolstoy used stylized supernatural creatures. In the melodious ballad, "The Tugarin Reptile," the Tartar hordes are symbolized by an enormous snake-like creature and in the poem, "The Dragon," the mythical animal represents man's unhappiness.

Tolstoy's belief in spiritualism was only one of the things he had in common with his close friend Emperor Alexander II. The ruler and the writer had been friends since their youth. In 1825 Tolstoy was taken by his uncle A.A. Perovsky, who wrote under the pseudonym Pogorelsky, to St. Petersburg. Through family connections, the youth became a playmate of the future tsar. Zhukovsky, the royal tutor, was also a friend of Perovsky. The young Tolstoy and Alexander were brought together on many occasions and a close friendship developed which was to last all of their lives.[64] In later years when Alexander was emperor, he visited Tolstoy at his estate Krasnyi Rog, and the writer had permission to enter the royal apartments in the Winter Palace whenever he chose. Tolstoy never took advantage of his friend by asking favors for himself. He did attend séances in the royal palace with the imperial family. While authors such as A.K. Tolstoy place spiritualism on a par with empirical reality, by the end of Alexander II's reign the occult science had also become a subject for parody

N.S. Leskov

The noted writer N.S. Leskov used supernatural folk superstitions and legends in his literary works, for instance, the well-known story "The Lady Macbeth of the Mtsensk District." But he also wrote stories that made fun of the public's interest in spiritualism. Three of his tales show his laughter and ridicule. “The Spirit of Mrs. Genlis” (1881) revealed the absurdity of believing that the spirit of a writer can direct the training of a young girl. “A Small Mistake” (1881) was a play on names. A woman went to an insane man and asked him to give her daughter Kapitolina a child, but through a misunderstanding, the name given to the raving man was the woman’s unmarried daughter Katerina, who, unfortunately, did become pregnant. “The Ghost in the Engineering Palace” (1882) was only an ill woman who, dressed in white, had come to visit her husband’s corpse. Leskov’s humor probably amused many intellectuals, but the reign of Alexander III saw a wide development of spiritualistic circles and the occult sciences grew with tremendous momentum during the rest of the time that remained to the Romanov dynasty.

Part V

The Reign of Alexander III: Spiritualism on a Par with Empirical Reality

In contrast to the romantic influences in the education of his father Alexander II, the future Alexander III had a very formal and restricted upbringing under the tutelage of the arch- conservative Constantine Pobedonostsev. The teacher, a ruthless authoritarian and estimable intellectual, impressed his own character on his student, a child of limited intellectual abilities. When Alexander became heir to the throne through the death of his brother Nicholas, Pobedonostsev continued as his advisor, a relationship that continued for the rest of Alexander's life.[1] After the tsarevich married his deceased brother's fiancée, Princess Dagmar of Denmark, he became more religious.[2] He and his wife, who accepted the Russian Orthodox Church, were eager for spiritual council, and developed an interest in spiritualism. Séances continued to be popular during Alexander III's reign and many such meetings had the patronage of the royal family. A spiritualistic gathering attended by members of the ruling hierarchy was held at the palace of Alexander's brother and reported in a journal as follows:

> "Hypnotic Séance of O.I. Feldman in the Palace of his Imperial Highness Grand Duke Vladimir Alexandrovich"
>
> "The séance started with experiments on the power of suggestion by Feldman and the Countess Shuvalov that great interest was immediately created among the participants. However, they were even more amazed at the experiments with hypnosis.
>
> "A young stocky and strong man served as the subject of the experiments. Mr. Feldman seated him on a stool in the middle of the reception room among the guests and asked him to look at the shining knob on his watch. Three minutes had not passed before the eyes of the subject began to blink and water; he slowly fell into a hypnotic sleep. Mr. Feldman said to him, 'Sleep soundly and don't wake up without my instruction.'
>
> "The young man fell completely under the power of the hypnotizer. Feldman began to suggest all sorts of illusions and hallucinations. According to the suggestions of Feldman, the young man imagined himself a captain of a fishing boat sailing out of Kronstat. The young man's eyes were open all the time. He acted out his duties as captain even during a storm in which all had to abandon ship. When the sloop he jumped into sank, the young man fell on the floor as if into water and then made motions as if he were swimming to shore. Once he reached the supposed land area, he shivered from cold. There he fought a bear

and screamed in horror. When he entered a tropical area he had to fight a tiger and a snake. It produced an amazing impression on all the witnesses.

"Before the young man was brought out of his trance, Mr. Feldman told him to take a silver spoon from the table and return it personally to the Grand Duke. After four days and at 5:30 p.m., the man appeared at the palace and asked with the greatest insistence to see his highness, the Grand Duke. When he was presented to the duke, he handed over the spoon and said that some sort of unexplainable force had led him there."

Because of the interest in spiritualism by the royal family and high society, as shown by the above séance, a journal named the *Rebus* was founded for the reporting of mediumistic activities and spiritualistic séances all over Russia. Amazingly, during years of political strife and social upheavals, the *Rebus* ran weekly, save for a few interruptions, for thirty-six years.

A journal that started its first editorial with "tra-la-la" and announced as its aim the printing of "something or nothing," "peach or war" and "cabbage or pineapple" would seem a joke that could not last more than a few issues. Yet the *Rebus* begun in 1881 did start with such a program and it published reports on strange occurrences and séances from all over the country until 1917. As a magazine that began on a whimsical note and became a serious organ for mediumistic activities, the *Rebus* was an indication of the widespread growth of spiritualism in the last half of the nineteenth century.

Reporting on the founding of the *Rebus* and about current spiritualistic affairs in Russia, Prince Adeka wrote the following to Mrs. Hardings Britten, the previously mentioned English spiritualist and collector of worldwide material about mediums:[4] "Since my last communication about the position of spiritualism in Russia, the occult science has evidently made favorable progress in the most influential quarters. The censorship has given its sanction to the publication of a weekly paper, the editor of which is Captain Pribytkov of the imperial navy who makes no secret of his being a spiritualist. I may say that his wife is an excellent medium for physical manifestations. They belong to the school of spiritualism which we call the American, which does not concern itself about reincarnation. The *Rebus*, for such is the title of the paper, has been out now for six months. Not wishing to criticize it, but the editor hitherto has dealt with spiritualism only in an incidental way, having regard to the nominal interest of the paper, which is understood to be in the discussion of rebuses, charades, etc. It announces that the profits, if any, are to go to the funds of a benevolent institution founded last year by Madame Pribytkov. This may have smoothed away some of the difficulties encountered by Captain Pribytkov in obtaining the sanction to publish. It may also account for the fact that half of the subscribers to the paper belong to the clerical ranks. Whatever the reason, the fact is, under all circumstances, significant."

The first editor of the *Rebus* V.I. Pribytkov, remained in charge of the journal for twenty-four years and used the slim profits of the publication to support a home for the needy. Anything that touched on the mysterious and esoteric was published. Mr. Pribytkov later made a list of the unusual events that were reported during the 1880s:

some examples during the reign of Alexander III are as follows:

> In 1883 in Diaghilev, near Riazan, all the utensils moved about in a peasant's hut. A pot of water went by itself from a stove toward the village priest and tossed water on everyone. The peasant burned her cottage with all her belongings.
>
> In 1884 in the apartment of the former military officer Florenskii in Kazan, potatoes flew out of a stove and dropped from the ceiling. After gathering up all the potatoes and locking the oven, the door flew open and more potatoes flew out. The police came and investigated, but the same thing happened while they were there.
>
> In 1884 in the apartment of Sukharov in Kazan, peas began falling from the ceiling when there were no peas in the house. That vegetable was joined by chips of bricks, boiled potatoes, underwear and military hats. Then things jumped up on cabinets and tables.

The incredible events listed above are, of course, of the tongue-in-cheek variety. One could even wish that the spirit in example two could have appeared in Ireland during the great potato famine. However, the above examples are a good indication of the sort of reporting that was done in the *Rebus* during its long history. More stress, however, was given to séances than to the sort of strange happenings mentioned above. Typical descriptions of séances are as follows:

Rebus June 16, 1885: "At Mrs. Makarov's several séances have been held. The medium, Mr. Galitsky, did not leave the group, but sat in the middle of a circle. The phenomena that took place were: 1. A wide golden bracelet with a strong dangling lock was taken without any noise from the arm of the medium. It was thrown on the floor and appeared unopened. 2. A box of matches was raised from a table and thrown on the floor. 3. Several words were etched on legal paper on a table. No one present touched the paper. 4. A rather small lady's suitcase lying on a couch, was transferred over our heads into the other part of the room, passing through a cotton drapery which divided the room into two parts."

The *Rebus* was not the only journal publishing accounts of séances. In Number 2631 of the *Novoe Vremia* (*New Time*) in 1885, the following account was presented: "During recent times followers of spiritualism have been holding spiritualistic séances, the number of which can be considered large. Ladies of the highest social circle at Pavlovsk are attracted to the circles. At these séances it has been reported that the young maiden B . . . has been acting as the medium. She belongs to a highly respected family. According to the stories circulating about her, she accomplishes feats that any medium would envy. She becomes sleepy and conjures visions of anyone so desired by those present. She also subordinates everyone to her will."

Along with the publication of séances in the *Rebus*, Mr. Pribytkov was very interested in events that could give verisimilitude to spiritualism. It was one thing to describe a séance, but it was more important to give the occasion veracity. For that reason, perhaps, séances that occurred in the homes of the aristocracy were frequently reported. If the ruling class supported mediums, then the assumption was made that spiritualistic activities were authentic. The editor also sought the support of intellectuals. In1889, Mr.

Pribytkov reported with obvious joy a conversation he had with the noted chemist, D.I. Mendeleev, who had denounced mediums in the investigation made by the University of St. Petersburg in 1875. At an evening party during a discussion of psychic phenomena, the editor asked the scientist:[5] "Do you now support the possibility of such phenomena?" The famous scientist said, "There are some . . . I've seen them . . . but they rarely occur. It doesn't pay to give them any attention and no serious man would bother with them."

Mr. Pribytkov was amazed that the scientist now admitted that such phenomena occurred and expressed surprise that Mendeleev felt that no one should bother with something that contradicts all the laws of nature. The professor gave the following response: "You know that ball-shaped lighting exists. This phenomenon is undoubtedly real, but what is the sense of it? It's a rare phenomenon and what serious and busy person can waste time studying it?"

Mr. Pribytkov pursued the subject and tried to make the chemist explain why spirits are a pointless subject of research. The exasperated scientist finally answered, "What you don't understand is, that one and the same are rubbish!" The conversation ended on that point, but the editor took pride in the fact that he had heard the famous scholar admit that he had seen spirits and had admitted their existence in spite of the stubborn skepticism he had shown toward mediumistic phenomena in 1875.

Mr. Pribytkov also pursued the activities of Helene Blavatskaia, one of the most notorious spiritualists in the latter nineteenth century. Her life was as unusual as her séances and weird fictional stories. Born in a noble family, she deserted her aristocratic surrounding and became a world traveler, a remarkable feat for a woman in the 1850s. She went to

Canada, the US, Mexico and India. She was the first Russian woman to enter Tibet and she even showed up in the army of Garibaldi at the Battle of Mentana in 1864. In the 1870s she became very interested in spiritualism and the occult. In New York City in 1873, she became the friend of several wealthy and influential Americans who helped further her studies in the occult sciences. In 1875 she founded the Theosophical Society which immediately attracted an enormous amount of attention and criticism. To escape the ridicule of the press, she and a Colonel Olcott went to India where they reorganized the society. Mrs. Blavatskaia did not lose her interest in spiritualism. She claimed that she could produce many spiritualistic phenomena without the aid of "spooks," as she referred to mediums. Stories of her cabbalistic spread far and wide and the Society of Psychical Research in London sent a representative to India to investigate her claims. He was not able to substantiate any of the incredible tales told about her, but he reported that her following was very large. Indeed, when she passed away, she had over a hundred thousand disciples all over the world.[6] In the 1880s Mrs. Blavatskaia returned to Russia and held séances in many cities. Mr. Pribytkov reported on an unusual occurrence that took place during one of her séances in the city of Pskov:[7] "In the reception room of the Ya family, many people gathered. They were followers of spiritualism. Leonard Gan, Mrs. Blavatskaia's brother, did not participate in the activity, but walked around and observed everything. He stopped behind the back of his sister and listened to her tales about the medium Mr. D.D. Hume who could make heavier objects lighter and lighter things heavier by his presence. 'And can you do that?' ironically asked the young man of his sister.

"'I have done it at times, but I cannot guarantee results,' coldly answered Mrs. Blavatskaia.

"'But would you try?' asked someone, and all insisted.

"'If you please, I'll try, but remember that my power is not equal to Mr. Hume's, and I can promise nothing. I shall look at that chess table. Whoever wishes to raise it now and afterwards, please do so.'

"One of the young people went and raised the little table as if it were a feather.

"'Fine! Now place it back and walk away from it.' The order was carried out and a silence reigned. All sat holding their breath and watched Mrs. Blavatskaia. She actually did nothing but stare at the table. Later, not lowering her blue eyes, she motioned with her hand for the young man to lift it. He went to the table and assuredly seized the table by the leg. It did not move. He took it with both hands. The table remained as if screwed to the floor. The young man sat down, grabbed a leg with both hands and began to nudge energetically the table with his shoulders . . . the table did not move."

Another psychic experience by Mrs. Blavatskaia was reported in the *Rebus* in 1884. The account was written by V. Soloviev, the philosopher whose interest in spiritualism will be discussed later. He had been in Paris where he witnessed the following scene:[8] "Several people including myself accidentally gathered at Mrs. E.P. Blavatskaia's about ten in the morning. The postman brought a letter for one of the hostess' relatives who stayed in the same apartment, but, as a result of the early hour, had not yet come from her room. The letter was placed by the postman on a table in the reception room where we were all assembled and where we could see him place it. Glancing at the stamp and the address of the letter, Mrs. Blavatskaia and her sister, V.P. Zh . . ., said that it was from their mutual relative in Odessa. The letter was definitely sealed in an envelope of thick paper which was impenetrable by the eye. Mrs. Blavatskaia (who was in an excited state that morning according to my observations) unexpectedly proposed that she read the letter in the sealed envelope. She then put the letter to her forehead and began with evident effort to speak loudly, writing down at the same time everything she was saying. When she finished, the sister expressed doubt at the success of the experience and said that certain details uttered by Blavatskaia could hardly be in the letter. Mrs. Blavatskaia became upset by the remarks and revealed that she would do more. She drew a sign on the paper with a red pencil and then underlined one word. Then with a strained expression her face, she pronounced with great effort of will, 'This sign must be at the end of the letter and this word is also underlined.'

Then they opened the letter: the contents of it appeared identical with what she had written, and, also, we saw a sign at the end exactly like the one she had drawn and the word was underlined as she had done.

"A description of what had occurred was written up and everyone in attendance signed it. The circumstances under which the phenomenon took place and all the slightest details testified by me, do not leave any doubt of their purity and reality. Deceit and tricks were out of the question."

Mrs. Blavatskaia wrote a book of short stories on sinister themes which was published in America under the title *Horror Tales*.[9] The story "The Ensouled Violin" is reminiscent of Dostoevsky's violin player in his work "Netochka Nezvanovna." While Mrs. Blavatskaia was well known at home and abroad for her séances and mysterious powers, the most famous name in Russia connected with spiritualism during the latter nineteenth century was A.N. Aksakov. The *Rebus* of course reported many of his activities.

A.N. Aksakov

Belonging to an old gentry family, Aleksander Nikolaevich Aksakov received his education in the Imperial Lyceum where he became engrossed in philosophical studies and spiritualism. In 1881 the London spiritualistic journal *The Medium and Daybreak*, wrote that from early youth Aksakov had investigated religious questions.[10] When he finished his courses at the lyceum, he wanted a better understanding of the Bible and studied Hebrew. Later maintaining that one cannot know the spiritual side of the body without understanding physiology, he studied anatomy and chemistry for two years. His work with the natural sciences led him to animal magnetism. During his study he translated into Russian a book by Count Shapari entitled *A Guide to Magnetism*, and published it in St. Petersburg in 1860.[11]

Becoming interested in the studies of the famous mystic Emanuel Swedenborg, in 1863 Aksakov printed in Leipzig a translation from Latin of *About Heaven and Hell from the Viewpoint of Swedenborg*. Later he also published *The Bible according to Swedenborg* and *The Rationalism of Swedenborg, An Investigation of His Teachings of the Holy Scriptures*."[12]

In 1867 and in the course of the next five years, Aksakov published the major English spiritualistic writings in a German translation. In 1874 he began a periodical in Germany entitled *Psychische Studien*, which was dedicated to theoretical and factual investigations of little known phenomena in psychic studies. His efforts in spreading spiritualism in Germany were rewarded by the praise of several famous scholars, including Emmanuel Fichte.[13]

In 1875 Aksakov traveled to England several times to view the work of mediums.[14] When he heard of the successes of Giuseppe Paladino I in Italy, Aksakov quickly rushed to Florence and invited scholars from all over Europe to witness the séances he set up. Everyone invited accepted the invitation and at the end of the meetings, they all signed a document affirming their belief in mediumistic powers.[15]

In an article entitled "Mediumistic Activities and Philosophy," Aksakov wrote about himself as follows, "What pertains to me personally is this: having never denied the possibility of so-called spiritualistic phenomena and holding to the truth that a person who is a witness in defense of the truth is obliged to do everything in his power to promote its investigation and acceptance, I steadfastly followed this path."[16] Aksakov's long and multiple efforts in his work for the promulgation of spiritualism were often recorded in the *Rebus*. For instance, when the noted journalist and historian M. P. Pogodin described a séance he had attended with Aksakov in his work "A Simple Talk About Wise Things" (1874), Aksakov wrote a rebuke to the description in an effort to correct the historian's memory. The meticulous notes taken by the spiritualist during the séance shows how diligently he approached spiritualistic matters. The *Rebus* printed Aksakov's rebuttal to the noted historian:[17] "In your 'Simple Talk about Wise Things,' there is a discussion about a meeting at Mr. Hume's. I consider it my duty to bring to your attention many details about this meeting which you no doubt have forgotten; otherwise it would be difficult to understand how you could have turned your attention to 'wise things' and then have written so superficially about something quite wise and which you witnessed. (A footnote from Pogodin stated that he had written down everything he remembered two days after the meeting.)

"You attended two séances at the home of the academician Butlerov. At the second séance the phenomena were stronger, more definite and so therefore I shall speak about them. As you were able to see, all that took place was written down by me at the moment it occurred at the same table behind which you were sitting; with the help of these notes, I can renovate all the details of what happened. We were not sitting behind a round table as you mentioned, but behind a common Lombard, opened table, covered with a common, flowered wool tablecloth. On one side sat Mr. Hume, opposite, Mr. Butlerov. On the left from Hume, you were sitting, then I; from his right, the Baroness M.A. L . . ., then the wife of Hume. It should be noted that the table was arranged that one side, free of legs was before Mr. Hume: one pair of the legs was by you and me, and the other pair by the ladies. The hands of all in attendance were placed on the table on which were located two candles, two bells, a harmonica and a pencil and paper. Soon the table shook rather strongly. Then it began to move and leaned one at a time in all four directions, not from one side only, as you wrote. This is necessary to note because Hume could have leaned the table toward himself, but he could not have easily leaned it to the right or left: that is, raise and lower it under our hands. That would have been impossible.

"After that, the whole table raised, all four legs at once, completely horizontal, about two or three inches from the floor and then smoothly lowered to its place. Then Mr. Hume proposed to those in attendance to test the table, and everyone was amazed that the table became at first exceedingly heavy and then extremely light while being raised on one side. If we assume that Hume strongly manipulated the table with his hands, even though everyone saw that he hardly touched the table with them, then how did he make the table become lighter than its own weight? You also recorded that sounds resounded as if they were strikes from something heavy on different points of the table. Then the strikes moved across the table and on to the floor. You raised the table cloth and looked at what was taking place under the table. I knocked with a finger on top and the same sounds resounded beside you. When you later placed your hands on the table, these sounds resounded with even greater force under your very hands. Then Mr. Hume, to convince you of the reality of the phenomena, sat beside you for several minutes behind a special round marble-topped table, so that you could see all his maneuvers. Lighter strokes were heard even on that little table. You wished for six strikes and six occurred. Then you and Hume returned to the larger table and events of a different sort took place.

"Hume took a harmonica, turned the keys downward and, holding it by the bottom with his hands, lowered it to the floor by his chair; his other hand remained on the table. The harmonica began to play and continued to play before our eyes. At that moment the tablecloth began to rise under your hands, touched the palm of your right hand and embraced it, as if by fingers from under the tablecloth. Professor Butlerov looked under the table at the playing harmonica and declared that he saw the clear contour of dark fingers on the keys of the harmonica. You revealed that something was tapping on your knee and that the sleeve on your right arm had been drawn back and then stretched out flat on your arm and held there. Then your sleeve was strongly pulled and you announced that a naked finger touched your hand between the sleeve and table . . . At that moment a large armchair on runners, standing by a large desk, a distance of two or three yards from where we were sitting began to move forward in a direction between Hume and you. Two times it raised itself up on its hind legs and still moved forward, moving up to the table by your leg . . . Meanwhile, the bell which you were holding over the table was taken from you and went to rest on an armchair. Another bell resounded strongly and for a long time under the table. It touched those around the table and finally fell into your hand. All the hands at that time were on the table. Then Hume fell into unconsciousness and the meeting came to an end.

"Well, here are those 'childish pranks' which you witnessed! Is it possible that a man of science, an observer, one who remembers the acorn fall on the nose of Newton, that such a one sees in these pranks an indication of nothing new in nature demanding further investigation? The London Dialectical Society designated a special commission four years ago which revealed in a published report that all these 'sham pranks' are real and the essence of actuality, but not explainable by contemporary science."

The spiritualist does not see anything supernatural in spiritualistic phenomena. He strives to find out and define the conditions in which they take place as well as the laws that govern them and the force by which they are created. By such means the field of psychology is being broadened.

Pogodin wrote a footnote for the above in which he commented that Mr. Aksakov was upset in vain because all that he (Pogodin) had witnessed at the séances was indeed childish pranks.[18]

Another eminent writer who criticized spiritualism and who received rebuke from Aksakov and others was the famous critic and writer N.N. Strakhov. The debate was opened by the critic in his book *The Battle with the West*, which contained three letters "About Spiritualism." The zoologist N.N. Wagner answered the letters with an article, "A Contained Philosophy," printed in the *Rebus* in 1883, numbers 42 and 43. Another rebuttal by Wagner, the article "Early and Unearthly Science," was published in *New Time* (number 2710), followed by an article further rebuking Strakhov by the biologist in A.M. Butlerov entitled, "The Possible and Impossible in Science." Strakhov waited six months before answering his famous critics. Finally he wrote "Another Letter about Spiritualism" in *New Time* (number 2848). The following excerpt brought forth a strong rebuttal from all concerned: "I maintain that in the sciences irrefutable laws, theorems and truths exist which are inviolable, in spite of any future investigations or observations. Few can find the center and radius of a science, that is, its true motivating forces, then we can easily determine the size of its sphere and is extremes. Then it will be clear as to what is located outside of it and some properties of that outside area will even be opened, for instance, some qualities which do not pertain to the area of known to us. Science does not comprehend that which is the most important: science does not comprehend life. The main part of our being is located outside of science which has nothing to do with fate, or what we designate as God, conscience, happiness, or personal worth.

"Irrefutable truths, which so frighten my opponents, do not have the value that they give them. The sphere or area described by them (under spiritualism) does not have that which is essential and precious for man, and the single excuse for spiritualists is concluded simply in vague striving."

Strakhov's remarks on science offended the scientists involved and N.N. Wagner replied in an article entitled "A

Dichotomous Philosophy: An Open Answer to the Letter of N. N. Strakhov." (*Rebus*, n. 26, 1884). Wagner wrote: "The inquiry made by you is in essence the following: Do we admit that there are irrefutable truths in science and by what signs can one discern such truths from the particular truths which allow exceptions. Before I shall answer this inquiry, I consider it necessary to explain a little about what you designate as truth. By the same formula of your question, you evidently create categories in truths as you do in everything else. For you there are general and particular truths. But the problem is not in that. The truth just doesn't exist as real or objective for you. You are surprised at the proposition I've put before you: that the truth is one and that it embraces everything in the universe.

"Now it is my turn to be amazed and put an exclamation mark: if you allow one truth, then how can you put up objections to others? And why did you ask us mediums what kind of irrefutable truths we admit in sciences? Maybe irrefutable truths, according to you, will be namely those which must be the truth for everyone. But in such a case, how can that agree with your revelation that the truth must be different for everyone—one's own personal truth? Your contradictions are not concluded in this alone. You defended irrefutable scientific truths in such a stormy inquiry that I now wonder if I can even consider myself a man of science or not. And suddenly you say the following: 'irrefutable truths, which scare my opponents, do not have the value which he gives them.' Now really; I certainly do not give them any value whatsoever and I am not the least bit afraid of them! . . . You say that miracles which cause us to be amazed and forces before which we must bow are more precious to you. This secret and precious region to man lies, by your definition, outside of science . . . In a word, you place science and its irrefutable truths higher than God."

Some months later Strakhov answered Wagner's attack and gave some of the most popular objections to spiritualism in the latter nineteenth century. Strakhov wrote:[19] "My opponents have caused me no small amount of difficulty. Being a great searcher for logic, definiteness and clarity, I presented a very precise question in regard to spiritualism: on what basis can we defer the possible from the impossible? I maintained that for the sake of a test, everything is possible, and therefore the test itself and by itself does not give us a source for contemplation and understanding; on the contrary, for the sake of speculation all sorts of things exist, and therefore, it is the fulcrum for our judgments and proofs. If I have three dimes in my pocket and, having decided to give them to a poverty-stricken person, I find only two, then on the basis of that test, I can conclude that it doesn't pay to give to the poor because such an act causes three pieces of money to turn into two. A similar absurdity would be like being in a forest where we would ceaselessly wander if speculation and common sense did not lead us out.

"Therefore I sincerely asked my opponents: Do not spiritualistic observations contradict certain clear aspects of common sense? And where is the limitation for speculative truth that cannot and does not have to reach any conclusions?

"With great effort I went through all of Wagner's analysis and showed that his mistake is in the fact that he does not understand the nature of speculation. Having no understanding about the real properties of speculation and yet to be discovered truths, which is the nucleus and basis of all sciences, spiritualists imagine that they can preach spiritualism in the name of science. I tried to show that in essence, spiritualism is a rebellion against science and that such a revolt is always an unsuccessful affair; that it is not only nonsense, but also unneeded nonsense.

"Trying to speak as precisely and understandably as possible, I explained that the truthful properties of a scientific conception, which has clear limitations, are evident by the area of its limitations. But my efforts were in vain.

"I have three opponents: 1. Professor Butlerov . . . 2. Professor Wagner . . . 3. Prince L.N. Tsertelev. The latter published a long brochure entitled: 'Spiritualism from the Viewpoint of Philosophy: An Answer to N.N. Strakhov, Mediumistic Activities and the Limitations of the Possible.' The main point of the author is that no philosophical study exists which could find it impossible to admit the truths of mediumistic phenomena.

"The whole point of the matter is that mediumistic phenomena contradict the laws of physics and chemistry . . . For instance, when mediumistic sounds of visions occur (spiritualists say), one cannot argue that these sounds and lights are spread by the same laws that govern the science of physics. Spiritualists say that mediumistic phenomena destroy the most important and basic laws of the physical world: the law of the preservation of properties and the law of the preservation of energy. (They say) the first law is destroyed by the materialization of spirits and that the law of the preservation of energy is destroyed by every display of the medium's talents. According to them, the smallest movement of a table, the slightest knock that resounds is already the destruction of the law of energy. A sound, as is known, takes place from the movement of material particles, and, consequently when there is no physical reason for such movement, then it is even more of a miracle, like the raising of a heavy table into the air by spirits.

"Thus, in the simplest spiritualistic experiments, phenomena occur which do not adhere to the laws of physics. That is how Butlerov understands the matter and its one of the amazing examples of how words can cover the sense of the matter. He stated such a view in Odessa on the 27th of August, 1883. He set their minds at rest in regards to spiritualism and claimed that the people of the scientific world had a moral duty to investigate this 'new wide region of knowledge.'

"This strange deception into which this very well meaning and excellent scholar has fallen and to which he is trying to attract others, is a result of an ancient manner of generalization . . . a type of generalization that could lead the world to chaos."

Strakhov's arguments certainly did not persuade the scientists involved to change their minds. Wagner and Butlerov were actively engaged in spiritualistic studies and experiments the rest of their lives. They were heralded by the writers and journalists who supported spiritualism because they were scientists who saw the occult science and a new science. This was the most popular belief of the latter nineteenth century. Tolstoy, as was shown, used the idea when he wanted to degrade his hero Vronsky in the novel *Anna Karenina*. However, other noted writers believed in the "new science," for instance the highly respected and noted journalist M.N. Katkov.

In *The Russian Herald* (Russkii Vestnik) in January 1883, an article about the conservative reactionary Katkov by N.A. Liubinov made some startling revelations:[20] "It was claimed that the noted journalist believed in spiritualistic phenomena and that they had a place in a new science. Katkov's philosophy, according to Lubinskii, allowed him to accept the church and aspects of mysticism, and he was especially impressed with the new occult science of spiritualism.

During the reign of Alexander III, spiritualism was popular among writers. For instance, the noted poet A. N. Apukhtin wrote a supernatural story on reincarnation entitled "Between Life and Death," and the radical writer V. G. Korolenko continued romantic stylization with his Jewish-devil-phantom in the story "Judgment Day."

I. P. Polonsky

The most noted author who supported spiritualism during this period was I. P. Polonsky whose interest in mediums began in the 1850s. After meeting the spiritualist Mr. D. D. Hume in Germany, Polonsky wrote to M.S. Shtakenshneider from Baden-Baden in 1857:[21] "I have made many acquaintances here and some of them are very interesting. For instance, at the Princess Butera's ball, I met Hume who so recently caused so much commotion in Parisian society. That magnetizer and warlock who communicates with the dead is a man of about medium height, white curly hair, and thin . . . He has frightened a lot of people here including the Princess Butera. While driving with her in a coach, he suddenly said to her, 'In five minutes a spirit will twist about,' and almost at once the old lady felt that something rough was rubbing her head and then her dress began to swell up roundly . . . She hit her head as she jumped in fright . . . this Hume invited me to visit him, so, I think I'll find time to do it."

Polonsky did become a close acquaintance with Hume and helped give the spiritualist a grand welcome in St. Petersburg. In Shtakenshneider's diary on November 5, 1860, there is the comment that during the evening "many talked about Hume and visions. Polonsky led the conversation. He has only one aim in life: to see his deceased wife either in a dream or in a vision.[22] Polonsky tended to attribute great meaning to spiritualism during his life and his literature shows his obsession with mystical forces.

In 1880 the author published his two-volume novel *Steep Mountains*.[23] The hero Peter Egorovich Klin, a seventeen-year-old student in the beginning, is strongly influenced by people who are predisposed to spiritualism. His former tutor Oznobin had a spiritualistic conception of women and was known as a mystic. In a conversation in chapter thirty-four, volume one, Peter declared himself a mystic like his former tutor. When he was told that a mystic believes in "that which doesn't exist," he replied as Polonsky probably did when someone belittled the occult science:

"Then every mathematician is a mystic because he believes in a point and a line in nature which do not exist. Everyone needs something that explains existence."

Another mystic in the book, General A.N. Oreshin, believed that the spirit of his deceased wife helped him in everything and visited him in his bedroom. Peter attributed the phenomenon to hallucinations, but in volume two, chapter forty-four, a glowing, eerie atmosphere around the general's deathbed causes Peter to accept the old man's dying words on the life of spirits after death. At the end of the novel *Up the Mountain* (1886), a sequel to *Steep Mountains*, the author mentions that the grave of General Oreshin is covered with grass, but as to whether his spirit hovers about the mound, "no one knows."[24]

In 1889 *On the Heights of Spiritualism* was published as an addition to an edition of Polonsky's works.[25] The book contained one of the oddest tales in nineteenth-century literature: "The Diary of David Dolgoglazov." While the story could be called science fiction, it also showed the author's predilection to spiritualism. Planets of weird spirits were described as well as reference to the medium Hume. The story served as a means of introducing the rest of the tales in the book, but as an introduction the story of David Dolgoglazov had little in common with the rest of the book.

Polonsky also wrote poetry that blended the supernatural with reality. The noted critic N.A. Dobroliubov explained the poet's use of the spiritualistic world as follows: "In the fantastic world, he found joy and relief from the squalor, oppression and deceit of life."[26] Polonsky might have been escaping from the dark realities of life, but there is no doubt that he accepted spiritualism along with others as a "new science" awaiting further investigation.

Not only were writers and scientists captivated with spiritualism by the end of the nineteenth century, but philosophers also showed an interest in the popular "new science." The social philosopher N. N. Strakhov's negative views have already been presented, but the opinions of the most noted Russian philosopher at the turn of the century, V.S. Soloviev, are of a different nature.

V. S. Soloviev

Known for his "God-man" theories, Soloviev approached spiritualism with introspection and caution. He was naturally interested in the "new science" because he himself had seen apparitions. His visions were as unusual as anything of supernatural nature in Russian literature. The vision of Sophia the Divine Wisdom first came to the philosopher when he was a child; secondly, when he was doing research in the British Museum; and lastly in the Egyptian desert.[27] Not since Pushkin's grandmother's "white lady" had a vision appeared so often. Soloviev's vision, however, was to have considerable influence on Russian letters. The Symbolist poets Andrei Bely (1880-1934) and Alexander Blok (1880-1921) were both interested in Soloviev's vision, which became for them the fulfillment of their search for a feminine mystique and for world revelation.[28] Much has been written on the influence on the Divine Sophis on Russian literature, but Soloviev's views on spiritualism itself are not too well known. He was curious about the supernatural and wrote an introduction to *The Vampire* by A. K. Tolstoy to prove that "the fantastic exists."[29]

Soloviev maintained that the fantastic had a place in literature because "everything that takes place in the world and especially in man's life depends . . . on some kind of causality." It was the causality factor that allowed the fantastic. Often real phenomena can have an unusual interpretation of understanding because of the chance advancement of facts or circumstances surrounding the phenomena. For example, in the story "The Vampire," Soloviev's causality factor is quite evident. In the beginning the hero, at a ball, was told that there were many vampires in attendance. Such an incredulous fact was difficult for the hero, Runevsky, to believe. However, he soon found out that he was told about the vampires by a man who was considered insane. Yet the hero had not disputed the information about the creatures when he was told about them. For a while he had accepted the news as fact. The fantastic had existed for him. There are other examples of the mistaken identity, etc., but they are logically explained.

In 1894, Soloviev discussed mediums in a review of A. N. Aksakov's book *Animism and Spiritism*. [30] From the article it is evident that the philosopher agreed with the nineteenth-century contention that the possibility of an unknown spiritual power exists, but he was opposed to the methods of mediums and considered their work a detriment to the discovery of the new spiritual force.[31] He felt that a scientific experiment has value when it can be repeated under its same conditions and for that to be possible, the conditions (1) must be known, (2) must be reduced to their simplest form and (3) must be under the direction of the person making the experiment. During a séance, the philosopher pointed out, the medium works with spirits which are (l) not known, (2) which are very complex and (3) which are never under the direction of the person making the experiment. In order for a séance to have any verisimilitude, he proposed that it be held under the following conditions: "on an open hilltop, on a clear summer day, in bathing costumes with the medium sewed up in a bag and curried in a freshly dug hole slightly covered with newly-cut boards."

Aksakov and Soloviev agreed and disagreed about aspects of spiritualism in open literary debate. In the *Rebus* in 1883 (n. 20), the editor Mr. Pribytkov enthusiastically announced the following: "With heartfelt pleasure we can include in this issue a phenomenon rarely met in periodicals: a peaceful competition between two opposing opinions in one and the same issue. The Moscow journal *Russia* (Rus) included in Number Seven an article by the famous doctor of Philosophy V. S. Soloviev entitled, 'About Our Worldly Heresies and About the Essence of the Church,' in which he briefly touched on spiritualism, without doubt admitting its factual side. In Number Nine of the journal, A.N. Aksakov's objections were given with simultaneous remarks by Soloviev."

The *Rebus* reproduced the articles by the two noted writers and the major points of their arguments are given below. Soloviev wrote: "Spiritualism does not satisfy man's religious demands by any subjective feeling and moral judgments, but seeks for itself objective support independent from us. And in this is the real truth of spiritualism and the only significance in it. Its misfortune is in the fact that the factual base which it wants to give religion, that is, those forces which act in spiritualistic phenomena, simply do not include in themselves anything of the sort that would be better and higher than we ourselves. Nothing about those spirits would raise us and make us better. In spiritualistic phenomena and discoveries, we stumble on the same limitation and inconstancy of mankind which we find in ourselves and from which we escape in religion. Spirits give to the religious feeling an objective support while being independent from it. It is good that they admit the necessity of such a support, but the one which they propose is not of value. The religious man can be guided by only that which is higher and more perfect than himself and which has significance without any doubts pertaining to it. There is nothing of the sort in spiritualism. In it everything is relative, everything is accidental and voluntary. The presence of inner significance in the phenomena and discoveries of spiritualism does not hinder them from being interesting subjects of scientific research, and this presence of inner significance and undoubted content makes them decisively incapable of serving as a base for true religion."

Soloviev later related that he was speaking about spiritualism only as a religious sect, and therefore criticizing it. However, when the occult science was referred to a "scientific research of certain exceptional phenomena of our psycho-physical world," then he admitted that spiritualism was undoubtedly useful.

Aksakov, as the major literary representative of Russian spiritualism, answered thusly to Soloviev's article: "What is spiritualism? First of all it is a series of phenomena existing in nature. It is an area of natural science itself. Perhaps it will be a widening of knowledge in all areas of nature, but for now it is found to be in contradiction with man's religious feeling or with that which ties man with the Godly. It's difficult to imagine how this can be. But spiritualism is not only a series of phenomena; its essence is also that incomprehensible conclusion, which is considered generally accepted as a result of the study of mentioned phenomena, that beyond this world there is admittedly existing another world which is just as realistic as the first and in which the spiritual-moral development of man eternally continues. Along with that, it admits that there is full solidarity of both worlds and their incessant mutual actions strengthen man in the sense that he is the incomprehensible link of the perfect and limitless whole.

"In the historical sense, there is not sufficient basis to see in spiritualism some kind of sect. Every sect has its founder, its leader, its teaching, its codes, its cults. Nothing of the sort exists in spiritualism, but as a matter of continuing to spread, it has not been spread by preaching, but by facts: not like a sect, but like a branch of knowledge. The nature of man is the code of spiritualism. Every spiritualistic experience is a new step and proof of the previous experience. What does this method have in common with sectarianism?

"In all countries where spiritualism is spreading, followers of it remain mainly members of their own religion, for it is compatible with all faiths, giving them only a more actual basis. There are Christian spirits and there are spirits that are deists with multiple shades of rationalism."

Aksakov and Soloviev were never to find agreement about the spirit world with which they were concerned. Sectarianism, considered by many the bane of the world's religions, was also a problem in the world of spirits. What the arguments of the two writers do show is the wide range of discussion that took place among intellectuals in the nineteenth century in regard to the world of spirits.

Spiritualism's advancement and popularity during the reign of Alexander III was a result of various forces. Members of the royal family itself attended séances, giving the meetings social approval on the highest level. The conservatism in the government after the assassination of Alexander II tightened censorship and put severe restrictions on political activity. Occult sciences gave many a new direction and interest during a repressive time. Scientists themselves were calling for further investigations into the "new science" of spiritualism. It seemed logical to the intellectual reasoning of many because Darwin had already shocked the nineteenth century with new areas of scientific research. Philosophers also investigate the spirits reported in the séances to find any religious significance in them. Social attitudes, science and politics all helped spread spiritualism during Alexander III's conservative reign.

Part VI

The Reign of Nicholas II: Mysticism and Seances in Russian Society and Literature

On October 20, 1893, Nicholas II became the tsar of all Russia, an event he had dreaded for years and a responsibility for which he was ill-prepared. Born on May 6, 1868, he spent his youth in the activities of a rural country boy: walking, skating, rowing, swimming and shooting. His education was sorely neglected. Under the tutelage of the autocratic Chief Procurator K.P. Pobedonostsev, the young tsarevich was surrounded by teachers of limited ability. He did come to the throne with knowledge of English, German and French, but with little preparation for the role he was to play in the country. A year before his accession, Tsar Alexander II described the heir as a "child who had only infantile judgments."[2] Considering the diary left by Nicholas, his father may have pictured him correctly. The future tsar never mentioned national emergencies such as the Russo-Japanese War of 1905, but did list carefully the number of crows he shot in the imperial gardens and, on September 27, 1894, less than a month before ascending the throne, he described a fight with chestnuts on the roof of the palace with Prince George of Greece.[3] Nicholas was too interested in out-of-doors activities to give much attention to the mystical and spiritualistic meetings among the royal family and in Russia at the time. However, after his marriage to Princess Alix of Hesse-Darmstadt, spiritualism was to play a role in his life.

Born June 5, 1872 at Darmstade, Princes Alix of Hesse lost her mother, the Princess Alice of England, when she was six. Reared largely in England at the court of her grandmother Queen Victoria, Alix accepted the ideas and discipline of the famous monarch. A picture of the old queen hung in one of the major salons of the palace at Tsarskoe Selo after the princess became the wife of Nicholas II. [4] The new empress spoke and wrote English better than any other language and her Russian household was run in an English manner. Imbued with the reserve typical of the English, the empress seemed aloof to the sociable Russians. However, she was also painfully shy and therefore ill at ease in her social obligations at court. A tendency towards mysticism had been evident in both her father's and mother's families.[5] Alix herself once called spiritualism "a sin,"[6] but in the time of her greatest distress, she turned to the occult science for comfort and inspiration. The empress's gradual sway to spiritualism is one of history's most intriguing and tragic stories.

Misfortune led the empress to spiritualism. When Tsar Alexander III was dying, the young, tall and beautiful princess was summoned to Russia in all haste so that the royal marriage could be consummated before the death of the sovereign. Her first appearance to the Russian people, however, was at the ruler's funeral and she became known as the "funeral bride."[7] An even greater mishap soon marred her image in the public's mind. When she and the tsar went to Moscow for the coronation festivities, a terrible catastrophe occurred on the Hodynsky Plain outside Moscow where a celebration was scheduled. Because of inadequate arrangements in the plan of events, several thousand people were crushed in the collapse of a grandstand and the panic afterwards. Not informed of the extent of the tragedy, the emperor and empress attended a ball in the evening, which aroused public anger at their "heartlessness." Unfortunately, the blame for the affair during the coronation was directed at the Grand Duke Sergey and the royal family was further embarrassed. Intrigues between the public and the royal house became common; and the royal family itself found little harmony among its own members. Alix wanted to please both factions by giving the country an heir to the throne. Four daughters born in succession gave her great disappointment until she finally had a son. Her joy, however, was soon turned to grief by the knowledge that the child was hemophilic, an ailment that she knew was carried in her own blood and passed on only to male children. The Tsarevich Alexis increased the empress's desire for isolation. She felt a need to protect him and deterred him as far as possible from any childish games and sports. Her concern over Alexis' health soon placed her in the hands of one of the most famous charlatans Russia was ever to produce, the monk Rasputin, who was destined to represent the folk tradition in the life of the rulers. His role in the emperor and empress' lives was foretold, however, by another charlatan, a French doctor name Philippe, who was to influence the mystically inclined monarchs and lead them to spiritualism. The Western supernatural and the folk culture tradition were again united.

Philippe, who was from Lyons, France, posed as a doctor of nervous diseases and practiced what he called "astral medicine."[8] He claimed he could fix the sex of children as well as other remarkable feats. He was introduced to Alix by the Grand Duchess Militsa, the wife of the Grand Duke Peter Nikolaevich. Philippe's attractive manner impressed the empress when she met him at Compiegne in 1901 during a visit to France. When the Imperial couple returned to Russia, Philippe accompanied them to the royal residence at Tsarskoe Selo. Séances were soon held in the palace and the doctor turned-medium tried to evoke Alexander III's spirit.[9] The immense authority the former emperor had always had over his son undoubtedly caused Nicholas and his wife to regard the proceedings with awe and concern. Philippe soon had the royal couple under his influence and the empress was strongly persuaded that she was pregnant in the autumn of 1902. She began to be disheartened with Philippe when she realized that she was not expecting and the French doctor was soon disgraced when he prophesied a quick success in the war with Japan. The disastrous war ended the foreigner's influence; however, before leaving for his homeland, he told the empress that she would soon have a second friend who would bring her word from God. He also gave her a bell with which to warn the emperor against those who wished to influence him.[10]

On November 1, 1905 Nicholas noted in his diary that today "we made the acquaintance of the man of God, Gregory, from the province of Tobolsk."[11] It was a significant insertion. The new "man of god" was destined to help lead the royal family to ruin and perdition. Born in 1871 in the village of Pokrovskoe in Siberia, Gregory was a self-proclaimed holy man who astounded his fellow peasants with his spiritual powers. It is assumed that he was capable of hypnosis because all accounts of his appearance stress his powerful, penetrating eyes. His surname was not Rasputin, a name which means "dissolute" in Russian; he was given that name by peasants when he indoctrinated them into his erotic and mystical doctrine. He believed that sexual indulgence was the true path to humility and through humility, one could reach eternal salvation.[12] When he went to St. Petersburg, he soon had a following among the sensation-hungry and neurotic society ladies. The same Grand Duchess Militsa, who had introduced the first "man of God" to the emperor and empress, also was responsible for bringing the second one to their attention. When the holy man first came to the Theological Academy, he was welcomed by Bishop Feofan, who was the confessor to the Empress.[13] The Grand Duchess Militsa considered Rasputin to be approved by the church and introduced him to the empress in the autumn of 1905.

Rasputin's relations with the empress and emperor reveal a scheming, clever charlatan who was well aware of the naiveté and mystical inclinations of the royal pair. In the beginning the rogue spoke roughly with them and never resorted to flattery.[14] The approach worked well and the brazen holy man captured the imagination of Alix. His hold on the empress was strengthened by his uncanny luck in being in the right place at the right time. Whenever the tsarevich was ill due to his hemophilia, Rasputin was so successful in stopping the bleeding of the child that he was able to convince the empress that her son was in danger if he, the holy man, was not heeded. Two amazing incidents have been reported in the memoirs of several personages connected with the court during this period. In 1912, while at a summer resort in Poland, Alexis fell while stepping out of a boat and bruised his groin against the gunwale. A serious crisis developed and the doctors declared themselves helpless. An operation was out of the question because of the internal bleeding. In their anxiety the royal parents telegraphed Rasputin. His reply came at once. "This illness is not as dangerous as it seems. Do not let the doctors torture him." The danger quickly subsided after the receipt of the holy man's message.[15] Again in December 1915, when the tsarevich was at the front with his father, another crisis developed and the boy was rushed back to St. Petersburg. The doctors again gave up all hope, but Rasputin came to the boy and the bleeding stopped.[16] Such miracles convinced the empress that God was working through her "friend" Gregory.

Actual meetings between the empress and Rasputin were relatively few considering the large influence the charlatan began exerting in political and governmental circles. However, he often communicated with her via letters which were given to the royal figure by her close friend and confidante, Anna Vrubova, the daughter of General Tanaev, the head of the royal chancery.

There is proof that the empress knew about the indecent activities of her holy man and that she took measures to protect him. She evidently preferred not to believe what she heard about her prophet. However, the general public and the aristocracy were well aware of the outrageous antics and vileness of the holy figure. Newspapers began to publish numerous accounts of Rasputin's orgies and wild parties. The press reforms of 1904 allowed the papers to print much material that had been banned previously by censorship. The empress, however, secured from the emperor an order that the news media must avoid printing derogatory news about the holy monk. The Ruler of All the Russians broke his own law so that his wife could protect their friend.[17] The incident did not stop public hostilities toward the charlatan for the leader of the Duma,

Alexander Guchkov, used the occasion for calling forth a public debate about the practices of Rasputin. So much adverse publicity took place that the tsar was urged by several governmental ministers to order the holy man from the capital. Prime Minister V.N. Kokovtsev followed the affair closely and to his surprise received a message from the figure in question himself. In his memoirs Kokovtsev writes:[18] "I was amazed to receive a letter from Rasputin. 'I am thinking of leaving forever,' he wrote, 'and would like to see you so as to exchange some ideas people talk much of nowadays. Say when. The address is 12 Kirochnaia, at Sazonov's.' Of course I have not retained his peculiar spelling. My first impulse was not to answer, but after some deliberation, I decided to receive Rasputin because my position obliged me not to avoid a man who had perturbed all Russia and also wanted to be able to give my personal impression of the holy man. Also, I was afraid I might incur the tsar's displeasure for refusing a man who had requested an interview. Finally, I hoped to be able to show Rasputin that he was digging a grave for the tsar and his authority.

"Having resolved to go through with the interview, I asked Mamontov, a lawyer in the Ministry of Education, to be present as a witness who would testify, in case of need, about what actually took place. I fixed on Wednesday evening, February 15. When Rasputin entered my study I was shocked by the repulsive expression in his eyes, deep-set and close to each other, small, gray in color. Rasputin kept them fixed on me for some time, as if he intended to hypnotize me or as if he were studying me on seeing me for the first time. Next he threw his head sharply back and studied the ceiling; then lowered his head and stared at the floor. All this was done in silence. As I had no idea how long this would continue, I said, 'You wanted to tell me something?'

"My words had no effect. Rasputin grinned a silly grin and muttered: 'Nothing, nothing, never mind. I was merely seeing how high the ceiling is.' And he continued to stare at the ceiling until Mamontov arrived. Mamontov greeted Rasputin and asked whether or not he really planned departing from the city. By way of an answer, Rasputin again fixed his cold, piercing little eyes on me and asked quietly, 'Well, shall I go? Life has been hard for me here. People make up stories about me.'

"'Indeed, you will do well to go away,' I replied. 'Whether people tell lies or the purest truth about you, you must recognize that this no place for you; you do harm to the tsar by appearing at the palace and especially by telling everybody about nearness to the imperial family.'

"'What do I tell? To whom? It is all lies, calumnies! I do not insist on going to the palace, they summon me!' he almost screamed.

"Mamontov stopped him quietly, 'What is the use of denying that you are the first one to spread tales. But the point is, this no place for you and it is certainly not seemly for you to say that you appoint and dismiss ministers. Think carefully and tell me truthfully why generals and high officials have been so nice to you? Is it not because you undertake to solicit in their favor? Did you not tell me that you had Sabler appointed chief procurator and did you not offer to speak to the tsar in order to secure a better position for me? I tell you if you do not leave the palace alone, it will be worse not only for yourself, but also for the tsar.'

"Rasputin listened to this with his eyes closed and head lowered, but did not answer a word.

"'Well," I asked, 'what are you going to do?'

"'Agreed,' he replied. 'I shall go. But mind, let them take care not to call me back since I am so bad I harm the tsar.'

"Such was my first meeting with Rasputin. In my estimation he was a typical Siberian tramp, a clever man who had trained himself for the role of a simpleton and a madman and who played his part according to a set formula. He did not believe his tricks himself, but had trained himself to certain mannerisms of conduct in order to deceive those who sincerely believe in all his oddities. Others, of course, merely pretended to admire him, hoping for privileges through him which could not be obtained in any other way."

Kokovtsev never talked with Rasputin again. He met him much later, but ignored him completely.[19] The prime minister's behavior toward the so-called holy man was not wise politically as he would soon learn with regret. The incidences that followed the governmental figure's interview with the "Siberian tramp" were as interesting as the meeting itself. Events quickly showed how powerful the humble monk actually was and how the royal family was so taken in by him. Kokovtsev continued:[20] "The next day . . . Mamontov told me that Rasputin had already reported at Tsarskoe Selo that he had seen me and that I had urged him to go to Pokrovskoe. He told me too that according to Rasputin, the latter's friends at the court were very angry. I determined therefore to report to the tsar on the very next morning and give my version of the interview. This I did. I attempted to persuade the ruler that only calamity could result if Rasputin were permitted to carry on as he had been doing. His majesty then asked me if it were true that I had told Rasputin that I would deport him if he refused to leave the capital. I denied having made any such statement. His majesty then said that he was glad. When he asked my impression of the 'little peasant,' I held back nothing. I added, however, that although I condemned Rasputin for his disreputable behavior, I condemned still more those who sought his protection and assistance. This practically concluded the audience. It was obvious that the whole business was distasteful to the tsar for he had spent most of the time looking out of the window. I believed it my duty, however, to say what I did. When I mentioned this to the tsar he expressed his appreciation of my sincere loyalty and devotion to duty.

"At about four o'clock that afternoon Mamontov telephoned that the substance of my morning's conversation with the tsar was already known to Rasputin. When I expressed surprise at the quickness with which the latter had obtained the information, Mamontov assured me that the tsar had had plenty of time to recount at lunch what I had said and that Madame Vrubova would have then telephoned Rasputin."

Rasputin actually did leave St. Petersburg the following week and Kokovtsev quickly learned of the royal family's displeasure. The next time he confronted the sovereigns, the empress turned her back on him. At the beginning of 1914, the prime minister was summarily dismissed with undue cause.[22] Russia lost an excellent statesman because of the wiles of ambitious politicians and the empress of Russia.

Rasputin returned to the capital after a few months and continued his riotous living. Members of the royal family tried desperately to convince the tsar that the vile holy man was harming the country. The Dowager Empress Marie Fedorovna begged her son to have the disreputable creature sent away. One grand duke after another sought to persuade the sovereign against the despicable intriguer who was using the royal couple for his own advantages.

Nothing, however, changed the opinion of the tsarina. Her mind was closed on the subject and she avoided the rest of the aristocracy, further alienating the royal family.

When rumors of World War I were spreading throughout the country, Rasputin sent the emperor a telegram asking "Papa" "not to plan war, for from that war will come the end of Russia and yourselves; we shall lose to the last man."[23] The tsar, however, had already started the mobilization that prepared his country for the ruinous conflict ahead. When in 1915 the tsar was at the front in charge of the army and the tsarina was in the palace at Tsarskoe Selo, Rasputin became the most powerful man in Russia. Evidence of the holy man's influence is seen in a commentary by the distinguished statesman Sir Bernard Peres who was at the Russian front at that time:[24] "Already in the autumn of 1915, it was clear that Rasputin was the most powerful man in Russia. For instance, General Mishchenko, with whom I was staying at the time, sent an A. D. C. to Petrograd to find out what was going wrong with army supplies, and the officer, who returned during my visit, explained that nothing at all could be done now without Rasputin's support. He did not assume the direction of affairs. He was still careful in his interventions, but that his approval was the first qualification for a ministerial post was already clear. The shame of this dominating led to protests from two honest servants of the emperor, General Dzhunkovsky and Prince Orlov. Rasputin had in the spring visited the tombs of the Metropolitans at Moscow and had spent the evening at the most notorious place of entertainment in the town, called by the name of Yar. Here he was both drunk and disorderly, and on being challenged used words which were deeply insulting to the Empress herself—'as to the old woman, I can do what I like.'"

Dzhunkovsky, we are told, presented the police record of this scene to the emperor, and he was thanked by being dismissed from all court appointments (September 8). Prince Orlov had more than once urged the dismissal of Rasputin. Now, we are told, he did so upon his knees, with the result that he was called upon to resign (September 15). Both of these episodes have several echoes in the empress's letters. One sees that the separation of the sovereigns from the people was gradually becoming complete. Even the Moscow nobility, given the imperial family and even the most loyal servants at the palace, were affronted. From that time on we read in the empress's letters as a kind of running comment on every appointment or dismissal, "He venerates our Friend" (that is Rasputin), or "He does not like our Friend."

Rasputin conducted the affairs of the country in a disruptive and dissolute manner. His reception room was always filled with charlatans and adventurers. His sexual exploits became infamous and his drunken orgies common knowledge. He was an outrage. The empress's friend Vrubova wrote that during the war crafty men "took advantage of his simplicity" and gave him too much to drink. [25] Séances were also part of his routine and a leader of the third and fourth Dumas, Vice President A. A. Protopopov, gained royal favor from attending spiritualistic meetings with the holy man. Protopopov was later appointed minister of the interior through the influence of Rasputin.[26] The governmental figure's political colleagues denounced him and refused to associate with him, but he stayed in office. When Protopopov began to show mental imbalance from work and strain, colleagues asked for his retirement. The emperor agreed and was planning for a dismissal of the ailing man in November, 1916; the empress, however, would not allow the change and a mentally unstable man continued as head of a ministry until the revolution. [27]

By the end of 1916, conditions in Russia at the front and in the rear were so bad that desperate solutions were needed. The famous murder of Rasputin was predicted by the holy man himself[28] and was carried out on December 30, 1916 by a group of highly placed personages. Prince Felix Yusupov, married to a niece of the tsar, invited the holy monk to his palace under the pretext of meeting his wife. Rasputin had shown an interest in the high born aristocrat and Yusupov took advantage of the monk's craving to entice him on a rendezvous. The Grand Duke Dmitry Pavlovich and the politician V.M. Puriskevich waited at the prince's. The three conspirators first tired to poison the holy priest, but the poison did not seem to affect him. Yusupov then shot the monk, but he managed to crawl outside the palace into a courtyard. Purishkevich then shot him again. The wounded monk was also beaten with heavy iron chains. Finally the conspirators threw the body into the Neva River where Rasputin drowned.

The last letter the empress wrote (Dec. 17, 1916) to the emperor before the latter returned from the front, reveals her concern over rumors that began to circulate around the capital:[29]

"My own beloved Sweetheart, . . . This evening there was a big scandal at Yusupov's house . . . a big meeting, Purishkevich, Dmitry, etc. all drunk. The police heard shots and Purishkevich ran out screaming to the police that our Friend was killed. Police searching and have not entered Yusupov's house—did not dare before as Dmitry was there.

"The police have sent for Dmitry. Felix wished to leave tonight for the Crimea. I begged Kalinin to stop him. Our

Friend was in good spirits but nervous these days . . . I cannot and won't believe he has been killed. God have mercy . . . such utter anguish. (I am calm and can't believe it) . . . Felix came to him often lately. Love and kisses. Sunny."

Rasputin was killed, and during this period of pathos in the life of the bereaved monarchs, spiritualism again played a role. When Rasputin's body was found in a tributary of the Neva River, a burial service was held on the grounds of the royal palace in the presence of the entire imperial family.[30] The emperor, who had returned from the front in time for the proceedings, spent two months in the palace cut off from almost everyone. The empress suffered great distress and agony. The Minister of the Interior Protopopov was one of her few guests at this time. He spent his evenings in spiritualistic séances in which he was supposed to have invoked the spirit of Rasputin.[31] The empress was naturally drawn to a man who could claim contact with the deceased "friend" and holy man. The power of an enormous country was in the hands of a distressed couple and a mentally deranged minister who had turned to spiritualism for help in directing that power. Revolution came naturally in a few months. Many forces led to the Emperor's abdication and exile. The final irony to the tragedy was that the royal family was assassinated in Siberia in the area where Rasputin had begun his rise to ignominious fame.

Besides the spiritualistic events in the lives of the royal family, spiritualism played a considerable role in Russian society during the reign of Nicholas II. Spiritualistic journals multiplied with such names as *Questions of Psychology and Spiritualism*, *The Amateur Phychic*, *From Dark to Light*, and *Questions of Psychology*. However, the journal *Rebus* proclaimed its twenty-fifth anniversary with jubilant self-praise.[32] The editor P.A. Christakos reminded the readers of such famous names as A.N. Aksakov, A.M. Butlerov, and N.F. Wagner. The editor also restated the aims of the journal and they were much more serious than the goals that were printed in the first issue of the journal in 1881.

"Our aims are as follows:

1. The collection, scientific investigation and study of psychic phenomena, psychology, mediums, animal magnetism, hypnotism, somnambulism, visions, spiritualism, spirits and so forth.
2. The spreading of propaganda about phenomena which are unacceptable to official science and about spiritualistic theories which indicate the incompleteness and error of materialistic interpretations of nature and man; that is, in other words, the *Rebus* has tried to introduce and popularize a world-wide acceptance of the spiritualistic view which is in sharp conflict with materialism."

In the same article of Number 52, 1906, the editor lists some of the proud achievements of the *Rebus* during its twenty-five years of publication. It formed the first official Circle for Investigations in the Area of Psychology in St. Petersburg, and in 1906 it created the Russian Spiritualistic Society for investigations in the Area of the Psychic, Spiritualism, and Experimental Psychology in Moscow. It organized and founded the First All-Russian Conference of Spiritualists in Moscow from October 20-27, 1906. A book of over three hundred pages was published on the meetings of the Moscow conference. It contained articles such as "The Case of the Immediate Letter," "Excerpts from the History of a Russian Mystic," "About Invisible Photography," "Astral Photography," "On the Upbringing and Culture of Mediums," "Radium and Vision," etc. Drawings and pictures accompanied many of the reports. The book proved that the conference was large, but it was not repeated.

Books on the subject of spiritualism were common during the reign of Nicholas II. Titles such as "Is Communication with the Dead Possible?" by Professor V. James and "Animal Magnetism as a Means of Healing" by K. K. Kudriavtsev were advertised in the *Rebus* along with many others. Books were also serialized in the journal, for instance, *A Dark Affair* ran over a year (1882) as well as *In Two Plans* (1916). Literature concerning the occult science was not written only by mediums or practitioners of spiritualism. Members of the intelligentsia at the turn of the century used spirits in their literary works.

A.P. Chekhov

One of the most prolific short story writers in Russian literature, A. P. Chekhov rarely used spirits or the supernatural in his works. In one of his early stories, "Perpetuum Mobile" (1884), there is a hint of an unknown force when a lawyer and a doctor are traveling together to a fair and the doctor says: "A strange, heavy foreboding is bothering me, as if some misfortune is hanging over me. And I believe in forebodings and I'm waiting. Anything can happen."

The descriptions of the weather in the story also add to the eerie atmosphere developed in the narrative. However, the "heavy foreboding" does not lead to anything supernatural. The story ends as one of the most sensual Chekhov ever wrote. A later story "The Black Monk" (1894) contains a black phantom which was based on one of the author's dreams. On January 25, 1894, Chekhov wrote to A.S. Suvorin and gave an interpretation of the spiritualistic element in the story: [33] "If an author describes a psychologically sick person; it does not mean that the author himself is sick. I wrote 'The Black Monk' without any dismal thoughts, just cold reasoning. A desire to describe a manic-depressive simply came to me. The same monk, being carried over a field, came to me in a dream, and I, when I awoke, I told Misha about him."

Many interpretations of the phantom monk have been given, [34] but it is evident from Chekhov's own description that the tale was not meant to have any spiritualistic meaning. The fantastic phantom is merely a symbol of the hero's mental imbalance.

The use of mysterious symbols was continued by the writer in his famous play "The Cherry Orchard" when the strange noise of a breaking string symbolizes the break in the lives of the heroes. However, the only story in which Chekhov openly wrote about spiritualism was "The Bride," but the author used the story as a means of deriding the occult science. The tale is about a young girl, Nadia, who is engaged to be married, but becomes a libertine instead of a bride. The girl's mother, Nina, was "occupied with spiritualism" and her preoccupations seemed to have mysterious meaning for her daughter. Chekhov belittled the mother through her esoteric interests.

Chekhov the pragmatist could not accept spiritualism and for that reason it played such a small role in his literature. How amused the great writer would have been if he had lived to read about his own spiritual appearance at a séance in 1912.[35] A Mrs. Maria Kiseleva, a writer of children's literature and the owner of a house where the Chekhov family spent the summer from 1885 to 1887, took a picture and a letter from Chekhov to a séance where the famous medium Mr. Wood Peters was performing. The spiritualist took the material in his hand and held it behind him. Mrs. Kiseleva described what happened: "Momentarily his face brightened up, not a trace of his weariness was noticeable and he began speaking freely and easily, 'This is a very capable, bright, thoughtful person. He is original, gay, witty and not hurried. Excessively sophisticated feelings. Loving childish, simple. He has been in the public's attention. He worked with pen or pencil . . . (Mr. Peters gave a description of Chekhov and many other details about the writer. Finally the medium came to the name.) I am receiving a name as if it were my own.'

Unfortunately, Mr. Peter's name was Alfred, not Anton, but the medium did write down only the letter "A." Mrs. Kiseleva also mentioned that Chekhov appeared at other séances.

While Chekhov did not accept spiritualism, other writers of his stature at the turn of the century did become engrossed with the occult science.

V.I. Briusov

In Russia during the 1890s, cultural changes took place which brought forth an aestheticism unparalleled previously in the country's long history. The arts were literally blooming, were idolized and were the *raison d'ê tre* of the intelligentsia. The Russian symbolist writers raised the level of poetical craftsmanship and held a mystical attitude towards the world. It was only natural that such writers would be drawn to spiritualism. Such a poet was V. I. Briusov, one of the leading symbolists of the time.

In 1900 in an article in the *Rebus* entitled "Methods of Mediums," Briusov spoke out strongly in support of spiritualism. Not only did the writer give evidence of his belief in the occult science, but he declared:[36] "We must stop down-grading mediums. We must read spiritualism as a science as we do astronomy and meteorology. Mediums give knowledge perhaps more important for people than all previous knowledge."

Later in 1901 in number 1026 of the *Rebus*, Briusov reported material that he considered important for the question, "Are somnambulists able to talk in languages which they don't know?" The write was quite taken with the occult and it influenced his literary endeavors.

When Briusov's first book of prose "The Equatorial Axis"[37] was published in1907, Alexander Blok wrote: "What a strange, magnetic book . . . (it is) a link in the chain of fantastic novels with an attempt at reality which runs through the nineteenth century."[38]

The use of the supernatural to enliven the realistic was a literary device in Briusov's prose of that period. The same technique was continued in the author's most famous prose work, "The Fiery Angel,"[39] a historical tale told by a German mercenary. The supernatural was used often in the novel for dramatic effect, and D.S. Mirsky called the book the best Russian work written on a foreign subject.[40]

Briusov was the only major writer at the turn of the century to support spiritualism openly, but other writers used spirits and visions as a matter of literary stylization.

D. S. Merezhkovsky

In their attempts to discover a new faith, D.S. Merezhkovsky and his wife, A. N. Gippius, a well-known poet, investigated spiritualism. Nicholas Berdiaev said that the couple lived in an "atmosphere of unhealthy, self-assertive mysticism."[41] Merezhkovsky used spirits in his novels for dramatic effect;

for instance, in *Alexander and the Decembrists*, the tsar saw a vision of Napoleon (part six, chapter two) and in *The Death of the Gods*, the Emperor Julian saw specters of the ancient titans (chapter thirteen). However, Merezhkovsky also presented spiritual beliefs of the Christian religion as spurious psychic phenomena. His technique followed L.Vax's suggestion in *La Seduction de L'etrange* that the resurrection of Christ could be the greatest ghost story ever told if the proper literary techniques were applied.[42] Merezhkovsky did use interesting literary situations. In his novel *The Death of the Gods*, a contrast was made between a magician and a Christian priest. Both were shown as sorcerers: the magician duped a crowd into believing that he performed a magical snake trick just as the priest fooled the faithful into believing spiritual rituals connected with church relics. Another example was in *The Romance of Leonardo da Vinci* (book thirteen, chapter twelve) where hell was chosen over heaven in a contest of visionary figures. Monks, slaves and cripples were presented in heaven because of the Christian principle "Blessed are the poor in spirit: for theirs is the Kingdom of Heaven." But when the visions of Homer, Plato and Marcus Aurelius were shown in hell, the dreaming hero asked to join them in the underworld.

Merezhkovsky's interest in mysticism and his search for a new religion was typical of the intellectual's dilemma at the turn of the century. This dilemma was also evident in the writings of symbolist poets who were influenced by the visions of V. Soloviev.

Symbolist Dramatists and Mysticism

The greatest symbolist poet, A.A. Blok, was possessed, as was mentioned before, with the vision of Sophia, the Divine

Wisdom, which was the subject of V.A. Soloviev's visions. The handsome, talented Blok crated his "Verses about the Beautiful Lady" as a result of his mystical contemplations about the vision.[43] Sophia represented a feminine hypostasis of the Supreme Being and he and his symbolist friends, Andrei Bely and Sergei Soloviev, awaited the coming of a new religious revelation through the influence of the divine vision.[44] Blok's mysticism did not last and in 1906 he wrote two plays, *The Balaganchik45* (The Puppet Showman) and *The Stranger46* which were a parody on his own mystical experience.

Other symbolists in their mystical searches turned to classical drama and wrote plays based on Greek and Roman legends. I. F. Annensky wrote *Thamira of the Cither or a Bacchie Tragedy* in 1913 which was based on the Apollonian myth of the proud harpist who lost his eyes by challenging a god to a contest in music.[47] V. I. Ivanov wanted to revive Byronic drama and have the audience participate.[48] The unreal and the real were to be blended together in the theater as in life.

Leonine Andreev emphasized his theme of death and nonentity in his play *The Life of Man* by having the stage darkened and dressing the actors as silhouettes which gradually emerged from the seemingly real into the unreal. He wanted "everything as in a dream."[49]

The mysticism of the time even entered political satire. A. V. Lunacharsky, who later became the first Soviet commissioner of education, wrote *Faust and the City* (1906) based on the famous work by Goethe.[50] The play gave an unusual ending to the Faust legend and abounded in supernatural effects: (1) a mystical white knight made various appearances; (2) Mephistopheles flew through windows carrying a harp; and (3) a strange female figure appeared in the sky and directed a chorus of spirits who warned Mephistopheles to leave the people alone.

The complex theatrical scene of pre-revolutionary Russia is a good example of the variety of philosophical thought that existed among the intelligentsia before the beginning of Soviet Russia. The mysticism of Blok and Andreev, the spiritualism of Briusov, the fanciful classicism of Annensky and the political satire of Lunacharsky reflect the diversity of the mystical experience among the *avant garde* of the period. It was a time of seeking and wonder in which minds sought refuge in the unknown, the supernatural and in spiritualism.

Spiritualism before the Revolution of 1917

It is estimated that before the great political upheaval in Russia in 1917 there were twenty thousand spiritualistic circles throughout the country.[51] The escapism of the intellectuals has been discussed in the developments in Russian drama during the period. The interest of the average person in spiritualism can be seen in the articles printed in the *Rebus* before 1917. Very little about the Great War was printed. An exception would be war advertising. In n. 21, 1914, the Grand Duke Alexander Mikhailovich published an advertisement asking for contributions for the navy and air force. His appeal against the "great enemy of Slavdom" which was trying to "encroach on our Dear Great Homeland" also encouraged young men to apply for training with the air force. A long list of banks accepting donations was also listed. The use of the *Rebus* for advertising by the grand duke indicates further the royal patronage of spiritualistic matters.

With the coming of the First World War, predictions from the spirit world began appearing regularly in the *Rebus*. In n. 28, 1914, a French spiritualist, Madame Thebe, predicted with complete assurance the following: "The war will last five months and fourteen days and a revolution will erupt in Berlin on December 4. On the 12th of December, the capital of Germany will be taken and on the 10th of January the French army will return home victorious."

From this prediction, it is evident that the spirit world was just about as misinformed as the real world concerning the length of the Great War. What is more interesting is that the article in the *Rebus* rarely even hinted at the catastrophic events happening in Russia. The country was suffering one of the greatest defeats in its history, yet the journal continued investigating the spirit world. For instance, after the above prediction in n. 28, 1914, an account of a séance in an upper-class home is given: "On the 27th of September, I set up a séance in a dark room at my home with the medium Ian Gusik. Besides me and one of my colleagues, my courier and servant were in attendance . . . After dinner I sat beside the medium. My mother soon revealed herself; her embraces were especially strong this time. She kissed me on the cheek and eyebrows; having seized my head with her hands, she moved it up and down, kissing first my forehead and then the top of my head. Then she seemed to stand beside me while placing her hand on my shoulder. I turned to her with a request—bring me, if it wasn't too difficult, some flowers. Not taking her hand from my shoulder, she made a movement with her fingers and her arm disappeared. Minutes didn't pass before I felt a little bouquet of leaves at my mouth. In the dark I could not see the flower . . . When I asked if mother could leave the flower she answered negatively by means of knocks."

In 1916, the year of incredibly monstrous catastrophes at the war front, the *Rebus* was publishing articles such as the above. Others appeared with names as follows: "The Dead are not Dying;" "An Unusual Dream" and "The Psychological Exhaustion of a Living Quarters." In issue 12, 1916, the journal advertised for its thirty-sixth year of publication, 1917. There is no indication of any apprehension about the upheavals that were soon to take place in the country. The *Rebus* did publish into its thirty-sixth year, discussing dreams, spirits and séances until the fall of the monarchy.

Epilogue

Both Russian society and literature were affected by the combination of Western occult sciences and the Russian folk tradition during the reigns of the tsars from the time of Catherine the Great to the Revolution of 1917. The Russian belief in spirits combined with the Western occult science brought charlatans into the highest court circles through the last hundred and fifty years of the Romanov's rule. Cagliostro was the subject of Catherine II's writings; the Baroness Krudener instructed Alexander I; D.D. Hume had the patronage of Alexander II and Nicholas II believed in Rasputin and Dr. Philippe. The tsars were influenced by the strong social forces: a folk tradition dating hundreds of years and a fervent search for historical and spiritual meaning among the Russian intelligentsia. Spiritualism answered the spiritual needs of many. Only Nicholas I broke the folk tradition that supported spiritualism, but his lack of interest only separated him more strongly from the mainstream of Russian life. It was as if the forces of folk culture and spiritualism were destined to blend together and contribute to the fall of the Russian Empire.

The development of Russian literature was also affected by the blending of the Western supernatural with the Russian folk tradition. In the eighteenth century, writers used the supernatural for philosophical inquiry and amusement. In the nineteenth century, romantic themes and images gave new dimensions to belles-lettres and spiritualism gave Russian literature a leit motif: the medium. At the end of the century, the supernatural served as a means of expressing mystical philosophical inquiries through esoteric symbols. Russian literature was enriched by the mysticism of its writers and by their acceptance or their adverse feeling toward spiritualism.

Perhaps the most important role that spiritualism played in Russian history was in regard to the philosophical dilemma of the Russian intellectual. In the eighteenth century, many educated Russians abandoned the Russian Orthodox religion and sought answers for philosophical questions in mystical sects. The Masons represented a sophisticated version of folk traditions during the period of the Enlightenment, a time known for the attempts to create systems, political or spiritual. By the end of the nineteenth century, the Russian intellectual was still seeking an answer to his break with the spiritual tradition. Dostoevsky asked major philosophical questions, but failed to find answers that satisfied many thinkers; Tolstoy was still seeking meaning in a world thought meaningless by many; and Chekhov showed his lack of philosophic originality. Disillusioned, people from all strata of society and professions turned to spiritualism as a means of escaping a world they did not understand, a world of pathos and war. Séances were held in the royal palaces and spiritualistic societies and journals flourished. The wide-spread development of the occult science is an example of the remoteness of tsarist leaders and society from the reality of the times. Spiritualism did play a role in the decline of Imperial Russia.

The occult sciences continued to play a role in Soviet society. In 1967 a conference was held in Moscow on the theme of ESP (Extra-sensory Perception); Sheila Ostrander and Lynn Schroeder, two Americans invited to the meetings, presented their findings in a book entitled *Psychic Discoveries behind the Iron Cutrain.*[51] The authors reported that Soviet scientists were asking the same philosophical questions that had led many intellectuals to spiritualism in the nineteenth century: "What is man?" "Do we have unused, undreamed of potentials?" In trying to answer these questions, Soviet investigations have brought about amazing amounts of research in Kirilian photography, telepathy, extra-sensory perception, suggestology and parapsychology. Vladimir Mutshall wrote in the American "Foreign Service Bulletin" (v.4, n.8), "If the Russian reports are even partly true, and if mind-to-mind thought transference can be used for such things as interplanetary communications or the guiding of interplanetary spacecraft, the reports will obviously have overwhelming significance. Soviet scientists are enthusiastic over their findings in computerized telepathy and in their studies of the lights photographed around human bodies. They ask, 'Are these lights the aura that psychics have long talked about?' And they exclaim, 'It's a fantastic alluring . . . world out there.' This Soviet research for another world or power can be seen as a continuation of the interest that caused the spread of séances and spiritualistic societies in the tsarist period of Russian history."

With the fall of communism in the 1990s, the Russian folk interest in the supernatural was again evident in the popularity of spiritualists and hypnotists. Anatoly Kaspirovsky became a public idol through his television shows and séances. Numerous imitators appeared in answer to the thirst for understanding that prevailed with the fall of the Soviet ideal world. The combination of the Russian folk tradition and the Western occult sciences has been a vital part of the development of Russian culture through the ages.

Endnotes

Part I

1. V. V. Sipovskii, *Ocherki iz Istorii Russkovo Romana* (St. Petersburg: Trud, 1910, V.I Part I A): 21-30.
2. Duke de Doudeauville, "Memoires de Ludwig XVIII," *Rebus*, (1885, N.23): 214.
3. M.T. Florinskii, *Russia: A History and an Interpretation*. (New York: The MacMillan Co., 1957), 505.
4. *Rebus*, (1887, n.20): 206.
5. S.M. Soloviev, "Istoriia Rossii s drevneishikh vremen." Sotsial'noekonomicheskoe literatury *Mysl*. (Moscow: 1964, v.15, ch. 29):102.
6. M. Chulkov, *Abevera: Russkikh Sueverii* (Moscow: Typographiia F. Gippius, 1789).
7. 7. I. Cooper Oakley, *The Count de Saint Germaine* (Blauvelt, NY: Rudolf Steiner Publishers, 1970), 19.
8. 8. *Drevniaia I Novaia Rossia* 1 (Jan-April 1875): 192.
9. G.P. Gooch, *Catherine the Great and Other Studies*. (New York: Longmans Green and Co., 1954), 87.
10. A.N. Pypin, *Istoriia Russkoi Literatury V. 4* (St. Petersburg: Tipografia N.M. Stasiulevicha, 1907), 136.
11. A.B. Kokorev, ed., *Khrestomatiia po Russkoi Literatury XVIII* (Moscow: Gosudarstvennoe Uchebno-Pedagogicheskoe Izdatel'stvo, 1961): 613.
12. *Cagliostro et Catherine II, La Satire Imperiale Contre le Mage*. (Paris: Les Editions des Champs Elysées, 1947), 49.
13. *Drevniaia I Novaia Rossia*, 194.

14. Ibid., 194.
15. Ibid., 195.
16. Ibid., 197.
17. Ibid., 196.
18. Ibid., 197.
19. Sipovskii, *Ocherki iz Istorii Russkovo Romana*, 313.
20. Ibid., 44
21. Ibid., 44 (Footnote)
22. Ibid., 23-24.
23. Ibid., 23.
24. Ibid., 26.
25. V.V. Sipovskii, *Iz istorii russkova romans I povestii: materially po bibliografii, istorii I teorii russkova romana* 18 (St. Petersburg: Imperatorskoi Akademii Nauk, 1903), 234.
26. Ibid., 215.
27. Ibid., 215.
28. V.V. Sipovskii, *Ocherki iz Istorii Russkovo Romana*, 82.
29. F. Emin, *Adskaia Pochta, ili Perpiski Khramonova besa s krivym*, (St. Petersburg).
30. G.A. Gukovskii, *Russkaia literature* 18 (Moscow: Gosudarstvennoe uchebno-pedagagicheskoe izdatel'stvo, 1930), 206-208.
31. I.A. Krylov, Sochineniia 1 (Moscow: Gosdudarstvennoe izdatel'stvo khudozhestvennoi literatury, 1955), 449.
32. Ibid., 48-49.
33. Sipovskii, *Ocherki iz Istorii Russkovo Romana* I, Part 2A, 78.
34. Ibid.
35. "Spectateur de Nord," 6 (1798): 205.

36. N.M. Karamzin, *Izbrannye socheneniia* (Moscow: Izdatel'stvo Khudozhestvennaia literatura, 1964) 661.
37. A.G. Cross, *N.M. Karamzin* (Carbondale, Ill.: Southern Illinois University Press, 1971), 113.
38. Ibid., 97.
39. Ibid., 111.
40. Ibid., 116.

Part II

1. D.H. Ovsianiko-Kulikovskii, ed., "Misticheskaia literature," Istoriia russkoi literatury XIX v., (Moscow: Typo-litogr Kushnerev, 1910), Volume 11, p.120.
2. Ibid., v.I, p. 117.
3. L. I. Strakhovski, *Alexander I of Russia* (New York: W.W. Horton Co., 1955), 175-176.
4. Ibid., 173-174.
5. H. Seton-Watson, *The Russian Empire:1801-1917* (Oxford: Clarendon Press, 1967), 166.
6. Florinskii, *Russia: A History and an Interpretation,* 630.
7. F.F. Vigel, *Vospominaniia* (Moscow: Katkov, 1865), v. 6, 39-39.
8. Florinskii, *Russia: A History and an Interpretation*, 630.
9. Ibid., 630.
10. Strakhovskii, *Alexander I of Russia,* 29.
11. H. Paleologue, *The Enigmatic Czar* (Conn: Archon Books, 1969), 162.
12. *Entsiklopedicheskii slovar* 4 (St. Petersburg: Brokgauz I Efron, 1893), 50.
13. Ibid., 50.
14. Ibid., 51.

15. Paleologue, *The Enigmatic Czar*, 130-131.
16. Strakhovskii, *Alexander I of Russia*, 65.
17. Ibid., 642.
18. Florinskii, *Russia: A History and an Interpretation,* 642.
19. Ibid., 642.
20. Prince de Metternich, *Memories, documents et ecrits* (New York: Stramans, 1884), 43.
21. *Entsiklopedicheskii slovar* 33, 176.
22. *Entsiklopedicheskii slovar* 40, 798.
23. *Entsiklopedicheskii slovar* 35, 9.
24. Ovsianiko-Kulikovskii, "Misticheskaia literature," 120.
25. Ibid., 118.
26. *Entsiklopedicheskii slovar* 72, 511-515.
27. Ovsianiko-Kulikovskii, "Misticheskaia literature," 120.
28. *Entsiklopedicheskii slovar* 9, 35.
29. *Entsiklopedicheskii slovar* 10, 723.
30. *Entsiklopedicheskii slovar* 6, 696-701.
31. *Entsiklopedicheskii slovar* 9, p. 51.
32. *Entsiklopedicheskii slovar*, 3A, 698.
33. Ibid., 699.
34. *Entsiklopedicheskii slovar* 9, 51.
35. Ibid.
36. Ibid.
37. Florinskii, *Russia: A History and an Interpretation*, 646.
38. *Entsiklopedicheskii slovar* 9, 51.
39. Ibid.
40. V.T. Narezhny, *Rossiiskii Zhilblaz, ili pokhozhdenniia kniazia Gavrily Simonovicha Christiskova, roman v*

shesti chastiakh (St. Petersburg: A. Smirdin, 1835), 173.
41. M. Summers, *The Vampire* (New Hyde Park, NY: University Books, 1960), 1.
42. A.R. Oliver, *Charles Nodier: Pilot of Romanticism* (Syracuse: Syracuse University Press, 1964), 88.
43. V.A. Belinskii, "O russkoi povesti I povesti g. gogolia" (1835) *Polnoe Sobranie sochinenii* 1 (Moscow: Akademia Nauk, 1953), 260.
44. C.E. Passage, *The Russian Hoffmanists* (The Hague, 1963) (Slavic printings and reprintings, Stanford University), 35-37.
45. *Poetry-satiriki knotsa* XVIII-nachala XIX v., (Leningrad: bibliotecka poeta, 1959), 304.
46. L. Pavlishchev, *Vospominaniia ob A.S. Pushkine* (Moscow: Universitetskaia, 1890), 35.
47. Ibid., 36.
48. Ibid., 37.
49. Ibid.
50. Ibid., 39.
51. H. Troyat, *Pushkin* (New York: Doubleday and Co., 1970), 117.
52. Ibid., 297.
53. Ibid., 290.
54. Ibid., 331.
55. A.S. Pushkin, *Polnoe sobranie sochinenii v desisti tomakh* 6 (Moscow: Izdatel'stvo Akademii Nauk SSSR, 1962), 773.
56. B.M. Eykhenbaum, "Problemy poeticki Pushkina," *Pushkin-Dostoevskii*, ed. A.K. Volynskii, (Petrograd, 1921), 76-96.

57. J.T. Shaw, *Studies of Russian and Polish Literature* (The Hague: Mouton, 1962), "The Conclusion of Pushkin's *Queen of Spades*."
58. Florinskii, *Russia: A History and an Interpretation*, 650.
59. Ibid.
60. Strakhovskii, *Alexander I of Russia*, 251.

Part III

1. C. de Grumwalk, *Tsar Nicholas I* (New York: Macmillan Co. 1955), 22.
2. Ibid., 24.
3. Adam Gielgud, ed. *Memoirs of Prince Adam Czartoryski and His Correspondence with Alexander I* (New York: Academic International, 1958), 102.
4. V.A. Zhukovskii, *Sochineniia* (St. Petersburg. 1885), 111-127.
5. Ibid., 120.
6. Ibid., 24.
7. E.H. Britten, *Nineteenth Century Miracles or Spirits and Their Work in Every Country of the Earth* (New York: Lovell and Co., 1884), 350.
8. N.V. Izmailov, "Fantasticheskaia povest," B.S. Melilakh, ed., *Russkaia povest* 19 (Leningrad: Izdatel'stvo Nauka, 1937), 135.
9. Florinskii, *Russia: A History and an Interpretation* 2, 812.
10. Ibid., 813.
11. Izmailov, "Fantasticheskaia povest," 140.
12. Ibid.
13. "Russkii Arkhiv 1," 1901.
14. "Rebus," 1901.

15. V.A. Xhukovskii, *Sobranie sochinenii* 11 (Moscow: Gosdudarstvennoe Izdatel'stvokhudozhestvennoi literatury, 1959), 237.
16. Passage, *The Russian Hoffmanists*, 36.
17. Izmailov, "Fantasticheskaia povest," 14l.
18. Ibid., 144.
19. Pushkin, *Polnoe sobranie sochinenii v desisti tomakh* 3, 13.
20. A. Pogorelskii, *Dvoinik ili moi vechera v malorossii, Monastyrka* (Moscow: Gosudarstvennoe izdatel'sctvoe khudozhestvennoi literatury,1960), 101-124.
21. *Entsiklopedicheskii slovar* 33, 348.
22. Ibid.
23. Ibid.
24. Meilakh, 145.
25. Ibid., 146.
26. Ibid.
27. O.M. Somov, *Povesti* (St. Petersburg, 1830), 73.
28. *Entskilopedicheskii slovar* 29, 531.
29. I. Ivanov-Razumnik, *Istoriia russkoi obshchestvennoi mysli* 1 (St. Petersburg: M. M. Stasiulevich, 1911), 89.
30. Russkaia povet 19, ed. Meilakh, 140.
31. I.A. Goncharov, *Oblomov* (Moscow: Gosudarstvennoe izdatel'stvo detskoi literatury, 1954), 105-152.
32. V. Setchkarev, *Gogol: His Life and Works* (New York: New York University Press, 1965), 119.
33. Ibid., 31.
34. Bernice Rosenthal, *Dmitri Sergeevich Merezhkovsky and the Silver Age* (The Hague: Martinus Nijhoff, 1975), 117.
35. Ibid., 118.
36. Ibid., 120.

37. N.V. Gogol, *Sochineniia* (Moscow: Gosudarstvennoe izdatel'stvo khudozhestvennoi litertury, 1959), 91.
38. Charles F. Turner, *Life and Genius of Gogol* (London: Gilbert and Remington, 1882; USA: Krous, 1971), 157.
39. Passage, *The Russian Hoffmanists*, 45.
40. H. Troyat, *L'Etrange Destin de Lermontov* (Paris: Librarie Plon, 1952), 175.
41. M. N. Lermontov, *Sobranie sochinenii* 1 (Moscow: Izdatel'stvo akademii nauk SSSR, 1959), 239.
42. M. N. Lermontov, *Sobranie sochinenii* 2 (Moscow: Izdatel'stvo akademii nauk SSSR, 1959), 504.
43. M. N. Lermontov, *Sobranie sochinenii* 4 (Moscow: Izdatel'stvo akademii nauk SSSR, 1959), 658.
44. Emma Gerstein, *Sud'ba Lermontova* (Moscow: Sovetskii pisatel, 1964), 242-23.
45. Ibid., 249.
46. Ibid., 248.
47. Ibid., 251.
48. K. Indostanskii, *Prizraki-okonchanie posveti Lermontova* (Moscow: I.N. Kushnerov, 1897).
49. A. V. Druzhinin, *Sobraie sochinenii A.V. Kruzhinina* 8 (St. Petersburg: Imperatorskoi Akademii nauk,1867).
50. A. V. Druzhinin, *Sobraie sochinenii A.V. Kruzhinina* 5 (St. Petersburg: Imperatorskoi Akademii nauk, 1867), 418-419.
51. P.N. Sakulin, *Iztoriii russkovo idealisma: kniaz' V.F. Odoevskii* (Moscow: Izdanie M.I. Sabashnikovykh, 1913), 281.
52. R. E. Matlaw, "Introduction," to V.F. Odoevskii, *Russian Nights* (New York: E.P. Dutton, 1965), 10.
53. Sakulin, *Iztoriii russkovo idealisma: kniaz' V.F. Odoevskii,* 280.

54. H. Troyat, *Pushkin*, 308.
55. Ibid., 323.

Part IV

1. A.F. Tiutchev, *Pri dvore dvkh imperatorov* (Moscow: M.S. Sabashnikov, 1928), 147.
2. S. Graham, *Tsar of Freedom* (New Haven: Yale University Press, 1935), 17.
3. Ibid., 18.
4. Ibid., 16.
5. Ibid., 19.
6. Ibid., 29.
7. Tiutchev, *Pri dvore dvkh imperatorov,* 147.
8. Madame D. Hume, *The Gift of D. D. Hume* (London: Trubner Co.,1890), 347.
9. E.C. McAleen, ed., *Dearest Isa: Robert Browing's Letters to Isabella,* 115.
10. Ibid., 116.
11. Ibid., 117.
12. Britten, *Nineteenth Century Miracles or Spirits and Their Work in Every Country of the Earth*, 251.
13. Ibid., 352.
14. Ibid., 351.
15. Ibid.
16. Hume, *The Gift of D. D. Hume*, 277.
17. Britten, *Nineteenth Century Miracles or Spirits and Their Work in Every Country of the Earth*, 354.
18. Ibid.
19. *Entskilopedicheskii slovar* 31, 224.
20. Britten, *Nineteenth Century Miracles or Spirits and Their Work in Every Country of the Earth*, 354.
21. Ibid.

22. Ibid., 359.
23. Ibid., 359.
24. Tolstoi, *Sobranie sochinenii* 4 (Moscow: Izdatel'stvo Khudozhestvennoi literatury, 1964), 114-115.
25. Tiutchev, *Pri dvore dvkh imperatorov*, 186.
26. I.S. Turgenev, *Polnoe sobranie sochineniia I pisem* (Moscow: Izdatel'stva Nauka, 1965), 470-471.
27. Ibid., 473-474.
28. Turgenev, *Polnoe sobranie sochineniia I pisem,* 164.
29. Rosanov, *Tvorchestvo Turgenev* (Moscow: 1920), 152.
30. Ibid., 154.
31. Ibid., 154.
32. Ibid., 158.
33. E. Wilson, "An Essay on Turgenev," *Ivan Turgenev: Literary Reminiscences and Autobiographical Fragments* (New York: Farrar, Straus, 1958), 57.
34. Turgenev, *Polnoe sobranie sochineniia I pisem*, 576.
35. Ibid., 249.
36. Ibid., 478-480.
37. Ibid., 80.
38. Wagner, *Po pofodu spiritism* (Vestnik Evropy, 1875), 860.
39. Tolstoy, *Polnoe sobranie sochinenii* (Moscow: 1963), 724.
40. Tolstoi, *Polnoe sobranie sochinenii*, 725.
41. Wagner, 868.
42. Tolstoi, *Polnoe sobranie sochinenii*, 345.
43. Ibid., 725.
44. Ibid., 727.
45. Ibid.
46. Ibid., 345.
47. F. Dostoevskii, *Pisma* (Moscow: Goslitizdat, 1959), 350.

48. Ibid., 350.
49. Ibid., 10-11.
50. *Rebus,* 230.
51. Ibid.
52. F.M. Dostoevskii, *Dnevnik pisatelia zo 1876 god* (Paris: YMCA Press, 1940), 139-140.
53. F. M. Dostoevskii, *Polnoe sobranie sochinenia v tritsati tomakh* (Leningrad: Izdatel'stvo Nauka, 1972), 293.
54. V. Astrov, "Dostoevskii on Edgar Allan Poe," *American Literature* (1942), 72.
55. Dostoevskii, *Polnoe sobranie*, 293.
56. P. I. Ogorodnikov, *Ot N'iu Iork do San Fransisko i obratno v Rossiiu* (St.Petersburg: Kolesova I Mikhin, 1872), 304-308.
57. Dostoevskii, *Polnoe sobranie*, 403.
58. Chulkov, *Abevera: russkikh sueverii*,
59. R.L. Belhnap, *The Structure of "The Brothers Karamazov"* (The Hague: Mouton & Co.), 34-40 (1975).
60. Dostoevskii, *Polnoe Sobranie*, 403.
61. Tiutchev, *Pri dvore dvkh imperatorov*, 148.
62. Tolstoi, *Sobranie sochinenii* (Moscow: Izdatel'stvo Khudoshestvenniia literatura,1964), 563.

Part V

1. Florinskii, *Russia: A History and an Interpretation,* 1088.
2. Ibid., 1086.
3. *Rebus*, (1899, n.12) 118.
4. Britten, 350.
5. *Rebus*, 3.

6. C. Wilson, The Occult: A History, (New York: Random House, 1971), 333-338.
7. *Rebus*, (1883, n.41): 366.
8. *Rebus*, (1884, n.26): 243.
9. H.P. Blavatskaia, *Horror Tales* (London: Theosophical Publishing House, 1898), 98.
10. *Rebus*, (1903, n.3): 25.
11. Ibid., 26.
12. Ibid., 26.
13. Ibid., 26.
14. Ibid., 26.
15. Ibid., 26.
16. Ibid., 26.
17. *Rebus*, (n.10, 1888): 99.
18. Ibid., 100.
19. *Rebus*, (n. 39, 1885):351-353.
20. *Rebus*, (n.16, 1888): 5.
21. "Golos minuvskego," (1919), 124.
22. E.A. Shtakenshneider, *Dnevik I zapiski* (Moscow: Academia, 1934), 518.
23. I. P. Polonskii, *Polnoe sobraie sochinenii* (St. Petersburg: Tipografia P. Galika, 1886), 8-9.
24. Ibid., 8.
25. I. P. Polonskii, *Na vysotakh spiritisma, Pribavlenie k polnomu Sobraniu cochenenii* (St. Petersburg: Tipografia I.N. Skorokhodova, 1889), 33.
26. Ibid., 34.
27. K. Mochulskii, *Vladimir Soloviev: Zhizn' I uchenie* 17 (Paris:YMCA Press, 1951), 64-76.
28. O.A. Maslenikov, *The Frenzied Poets* (Los Angeles: University of California Press, 1952), 62-63, 164-168.
29. A.K. Tolstoy, v. 3, 7-11.
30. Soloviev, *Istoriia Rossii s drevneishikh vremen,* 100.

31. Ibid., 112.
32. M.M. Petrovo-Solovova, *Mediumicheskiia fizicheskiia iavlenii I ikh nauchoe izsledovanie* (St. Petersburg: V. Demakov, 1900), 197.
33. Ibid., 199.

Part VI

1. Florinskii, *Russia: A History and an Interpretation* 2, 1141.
2. V. Cowles, *The Romanovs* (New York: Harper & Rowe, 1971), 235.
3. Florinskii, *Russia: A History and an Interpretation* 2, 1141.
4. B. Pares, *Letters of the Tsaritsa to the Tsar, 1914-l916* (New York: Robert M. McBride & Co., 1924), 9.
5. Ibid., 10.
6. Ibid., 14.
7. Ibid., 11.
8. Ibid., 14.
9. Ibid., 14.
10. Ibid., 15.
11. Florinskii, *Russia: A History and an Interpretation* 11, 1146.
12. Ibid., 1145.
13. Pares, *Letters of the Tsaritsa to the Tsar, 1914-l916,* 15.
14. Ibid., 15.
15. Ibid., 27.
16. Ibid., 27.
17. Ibid., 26.
18. V.N. Kokovtsov, *Out of My Past* (Stanford, CA: Stanford University Press, 1935), 296.

19. Ibid.
20. Ibid., 297.
21. Ibid., 418.
22. Pares, *Letters of the Tsaritsa to the Tsar, 1914-l916,* 20.
23. Ibid., 24.
24. Ibid., 31.
25. Ibid., 16.
26. Ibid., 36.
27. Ibid., 36.
28. Ibid., 11.
29. Kokovtsov, *Out of My Past,* 462.
30. Pares, *Letters of the Tsaritsa to the Tsar, 1914-l916,* 11.
31. Ibid., 12.
32. *Rebus*, (n. 52, 1906): p. 5
33. A.P. Chekhov, *Sobranie sochinenii v dbenadtsat' tomakh* (Moscow: Izdatil'stvo Khudozhestvenaia literature,1964), v. 12
34. T. Winner, *Chekhov and His Prose* (New York: Holt, Reinhart, 1966), 113.
35. *Rebus*, (1912, n. 15): 6.
36. *Rebus*, (1900, n. 38): 969.
37. *Briusovskie chteniia 1963 goda* (Yerevan: Aristan," 1964), 101.
38. V. Briusov, *Republic of the Southern Cross* (New York: McBride, 1920), p. 84.
39. V. Briusov, *Sobrania soschinenii* (Moscow: Nauka, 1974), p. 57.
40. D.S. Mirskii, *Contemporary Russian Literature, 1881-1925* (New York: A. Knopf, 1926), 190.
41. N. Berdiaev, *Dream and Reality* (New York: McMillan, 1951), 144.

42. L.Vax, *La Seduction de l'strange* (Paris: U de France, 1965), 60.
43. Maslenikov, *The Frenzied Poets,* 154.
44. Ibid.
45. M.L. Hoover, *Meyerhold: The Art of Conscious Theater* (Amherst: University of Massachusetts Press, 1974), 9.
46. Mirskii, *Contemporary Literature*,216-217.
47. Ibid., 202-205.
48. Ibid., 205- 209.
49. Meyerhold, 9, 26, 38, 40.
50. Mirskii, *Contemporary Literature*, 361.
51. S. Ostrander and L. Schroeder, *Psychic Discoveries behind the Iron Curtain* (Englewood Cliffs, NJ: Prentice-Hall, 1970), 230.

Selected Bibliography

Astrov, V. "F. Dostoevsky and Edgar Allan Poe," *American Literature*. 1942.

V. Belinskii. "O russkoi povesti i sobranie sochinenii." *Polnoe sobranie.* Moscow, 1953.

Berdiaev, N. *Dream and Reality*. New York: 1951.

Blavatskaia, H.P. *Horror Tales.* London: 1891.

Britten, E. H. *Nineteenth-Century Miracles: or Spirits and Their Work.* New York: 1884.

Briusov, V. *The Republic of the Southern Cross and Other Stories.* New York: 1920.

Briusov, V. *Sobranie sochinenii.* Moscow: 1974. *Briusovskie chteniia 1963 goda,* (Yerevan, 1964)

Chekhov, A.P. *Sobranie sochinenii v dvenadtsat' tomak.,* Moscow: 1964.

Chulkov, M. *Abevera:Russkikh sueverii.* Moscow: 1789.

Cooper Oakley, I. *Count de Saint Germaine.* New York: 1970.

Cowles, Virginia. *The Romanov.,* New York: 1971.

Cross, A.G. *N. M. Karamzi.* Carbondale, Ill. : 1971.

Dostoevskii, F.M. *Polnoe sobranie sochinenia v tridtsati tomakh*. Leningrad: 1971.

Dostoevskii, F.M. *Dnevnik pisatelia pa 1876 god.* Paris: 1940.

Dostoevskii, F.M. *Pis'ma*. Moscow: 1959.

Druzhnin, A.V. *Sobranie sochinenii.* St. Petersburg: 1867.

Emin, F. *Adskaia Pochta.* St. Petersburg:1780.

Entsiklopedicheskii slovar, Brokgauz I Efron: 1893.

Eikhenbaum, B.M. *Problemy poetiki Pushkina.* Petrograd: 1921.
Florinskii, M.T. *Russia: A History and an Interpretation.* New York: 1957.
Gerstein, Emma. *Sud'ba Lermontova.* Moscow: 1964.
Gielgud, A. E. *Memoirs of Prince Adam Czartoryski.* New York: 1968.
Gogol, N.V. *Sochineniia.* Moscow: 1959.
Goncharov, I.A. *Oblomov.* Moscow: 1954.
Gooch, G.P. *Catherine the Great.* New York: 1954.
Graham, S. *Tsar of Freedom.* New Haven, 1935.
Gukovskii, G. A. *Russkaiia literature.* Moscow: 1939.
Home (Hume), Mrs. D. *The Gift of D.D. Home.* London: 1890.
Hoover, M.L. *Meyerhold: the Art of Conscious Theater.* Amherst: 1974.
Indostanskii, K. *Prizraki-okonchanie povesti Lermontova.* Moscow:1897.
Ivanov-Razumnik, I. *Istoriia russkoi obshchestvennoi mysli.* (St. Petersburg, 1911).
Izmailov, N.V. *Fantasticheskaia russkaia posvest' XIX veka.* Leningrad: 1973.
Karamzin, N.M. *Izbrannye sochenniia.* Moscow: 1964.
Kokorev, A.B., ed. *Khrestomatiia po russkoi literatury XVIII veka.* Moscow: 1961.
Kokovtsov, V.N. *Out of My Past.* Stanford: 1935.
Krylov, I.A. *Sochineniia*. Moscow: 1955.
Lermontov, M. I. *Sobranie sochinenii*. Moscow: 1959.
Lirondelle, L. *Le Poete Alexis Tolstoi.* Paris, 1912.
Maslenikov, O.A. *The Frenzied Poets.* Los Angeles: 1952.
Matlaw, R.E. "Introduction," V.F. Odoevskii, *Russian Nights*. New York: 1965.

McAleen, E.C., ed. *Dearest Isa: Robert Browning's Letters to Isabella Blagden*. Austin: 1951.

Metternich, Prince de. *Memoires.* New York: 1884.

Mirskii, D. S. *Contemporary Russian Literature, 1881-1925.* New York: 1926.

Mochulskii, K. *Vladimir Soloviev.* Paris: 1951.

Narezhny, V.T. *Rossiiskii Zhilblaz.* St. Petersburg: 1835.

Ogorodnikov, P.I., *Ot N'iu Iorka doSan Frantsisko I obratno.* St. Petersburg: 1972.

Oliver, A.R. *Charles Nodier:Pilot of Romanticism.* Syracuse: 1964.

Ovsianiko-Kulikovskii, D.H., ed. "*Misticheskaia literature,*" *Istoriia Russkoi Literatury* 19. Moscow:1910.

Ostrander, S. and L. Schroeder. *Psychic Discoveries behind the Iron Curtain.* Englewood Cliffs, NJ: 1970.

Paleologue, M. *The Enigmatic Czar.* Hamden, Conn.: 1969.

Pares, Sir Bernard. *Letters of the Tsaritsa to the Tsar.* New York: 1924.

Passage, C.E. *The Russian Hoffmannists*. The Hague: 1963.

Pavlishchev, L. *Vospominaniia ob A.S. Pushkine.* Moscow: 1890.

Petrovo-Solovovo, M.M. *Mediumicheskiia fizicheskiia iavleniia.* St.Petersburg:1900.

Pogorelskii, A. *Dvoinik ili moi vechera v malorossi*. Moscow: 1960.

Polonskii, I.P. *Na vysotakh spiritizma.* St.Petersburg: 1889.

Pushkin, A.S. *Polnoe sobranie sochinenii v desiasti nomakh*. Moscow: 1862.

Pypin, A.N. *Istoriia russkoi literatury.* St. Petersburg: 1907.

Rosenthal, B. *D.S. Merezhkovsky and the Silver Age.* The Hague: 1975.

Rosanov, I.N. *Tvorchestvo Turgeneva.* Moscow:1920.

Sakulin, P.N. *Iz istorii russkogo idealisma: V.F. Odoevskii.* Moscow: 1913.

Setchkarev, V. *Gogol: His Life and Works.* New York: 1965.

Seton-Watson, H. *Therussian Empire:1801-1917.* Oxford: 1967.

Shaw, J.T. "The Conclusion of Pushkin's 'Queen of Spades'" in *Studies of Russian and Polish Literature.* The Hague: 1962.

Shtakenshneider, E.A. *Dnevnik I zapiski.* Moscow: 1934.

Sipovskii, V.V. *Iz istorii russkogo bibliografii, istorii I teorii russkogo romana.* St. Petersburg: 1903.

Soloviev, S.M. *Istoriia Rossii s drevneishikh vremen.* Moscow: 1964.

Somov, O.M. *Povesti.* St. Petersburg: 1830.

Strakhovskii, L.I. *Alelxander I of Russia.* New York: 1955.

Summers, M. *The Vampire.* New York: 1960.

Tolstoi, A.K. *Polnoe sobranie sochinenii.* St. Petersburg: 1907.

Tolstoi, A.K. *Sobranie sochinenii.* Moscow: 1964.

Tolstoi, L.N. *Polnoe sobranie sochinenii.* Moscow 1963.

Troyat, H. *L'E'trange destin de Lermontov.* Paris: 1952.

Troyat, H. *Pushkine.* New York: 1970.

Turgenev, I.S. *Polnoe sobranie sochineniia.* Moscow: 1965.

Turner, C.F. *Life and Genius of Gogol.* London: 1971.

Tiutchev, A.F. *Pri dvore dvkh imperatorov.* Moscow:1928.

Wilson C. *The Occult.* New York: 1971.

Wilson, E. *Ivan Turgenev, Literary Reminiscences*(London, Faber & faber, 1959) p.69.

Winner, T. *Chekhov and his Prose.* New York: 1966.

Vax, L. *La Séduction de l'é trange*. Paris: 1965.
Vigel, F.F. *Vospominaniia*. Moscow : 1865.
Zhukovskii, V.A. *Sobranie sochinenii*. Moscow:1959.

Lightning Source UK Ltd.
Milton Keynes UK
UKOW05f1023130813

215261UK00003B/68/P